LIFE IN AMERICA

Also:
Diamond Boy
My Father's Tale

LIFE IN AMERICA

Savann T. Mey

Library of Congress Control Number:		2008904198
ISBN:	Hardcover	978-1-4363-4187-5
	Softcover	978-1-4363-4186-8

To order additional copies of this book, contact:
Xlibris Corporation
1-888-795-4274
www.Xlibris.com
Orders@Xlibris.com
48705

DEDICATION

To my daughter, Cryxtal Sophary-Mey Sokhan

ACKNOWLEDGMENTS

Washington State Trooper Guy Gill number 505,

Thank you for your professionalism, also for the teddy bear to lift up the spirits of my Cryxtal and Diamond. I really appreciated the hot cocoa for my children and the coffee for myself. Also to his partner, the one with the smokes coming out of the hood of his cruiser on the night before Martin Luther King's birthday. He has to ask Mr. Guy Gill to transfer us to Shari's in Olympia, Washington, of 2008.

Ms. Desiree of Shari's Restaurant, on Martin,

Thanks for the breakfast for my Cryxtal and Diamond; we really appreciated the hospitality and for going out of your way to make us comfortable.

Mr. Don Woods,

Thank you for the gas; we appreciated your help, and it was nice meeting your wife. I like your house.

Thanks also to the Caucasian man that refused to help us out because if he would have helped, we would have missed the opportunity of Mr. Wood helping us out, and we wouldn't have enough gas to get where we need to go. I know it's you, Mr. Wood, who filled up my tank. Thanks!

My best friend, Keo Savongxay. Thank you for your encouragement and your special friendship, my little God's sister Sumolly Dam. And, Sarita out of Stockton, the one that would be the best for me, where you at?

CHAPTER 1

Life in America is different for me; and at the beginning, there's no doubt. I was sure I'll have a future here in America, but my hope died as quickly as it sprung up. Everything started so quick and fast for me that I didn't see myself on the fast lane, and I run into different types of problems and troubles. It wasn't bad back in Lawton where Father Robert guided my every step, teaching me how to walk and talk; but after my relocation to California (during this time I was residing here in Modesto), I ran into all kinds of danger, putting my health and safety at risk. No matter what I do, nothing came out as I have planned. But at the same time, I refused to let myself accept any belief of defeat or thoughts of failure in my mistakes; and in my worst situation, I took advantage of my present life and worked toward the good and better of the future. Coming out of the dungeon after serving my prison sentence, I have all the experience and the skills that I needed to overcome my predicament, on top of the worst condition known to humankind. I have learned to master all obstacles that ever crossed my path. And part of it because I didn't raise my hand up and quit fighting. Even when everything seemed hopeless, I keep faithfully struggling on, never giving up; and like out of the mist of the killing field, I made it to America by the kindness of my supposed-to-be wife Kimberly's sponsorship that saved my life and that I lived. Only if she didn't return back to Cambodia to have the chopper she was on crash, and die, she's the best for me. And I don't understand why she had to go to her death and leave me to be reunited with Chantho (who only caused me more harm than good). I curse the day that I ran into her; but at the same time I also feel blessed that we met, because if we never ran into each other, I don't think I would be the man that I am today, whether for better or worse. She has taken part in the molding and the creating of who I am today.

CHAPTER 2

Living in Lawton, Oklahoma, everything was mellow. And the people there are easygoing, including Father Robert and my supposed-to-be wife, Kimberly. I was eighteen years old, and my name has been changed from Athom to Tommy; and since I don't have a last name nor do I know it, Kimberly thought that it's a good idea to use the name of the state that I am going to live my life for my new last name, and that's how the Ok come about, the abbreviation for Oklahoma with Lawton as my middle name as a reminder that that's where I was reborn. Actually, all the time that I was with Kimberly, I didn't understand most of the things that she's talking about, but I have learned early on to just go with the flow and let the pro do the job because they knew better. 'Til today, I'm not sure if Kimberly's love for me was pure and true or not; I'm not sure if she decided to marry me because she has a good heart and wanted to help me out of my danger. But she's a priest's daughter. So there isn't any telling. On top of everything else, she's from America, where everyone is free and has the liberty to doing anything that one wishes—good or bad, right or wrong, you create your world. You can make it paradise on earth or a forever-burning hell behind bar in a prison cell.

I was being shown around the house by Father Robert while my wife stacked the refrigerator and was putting all the supplies and canned goods away in the cabinets. I was excited beyond words, and my eyes couldn't see enough. Exiting through the side of the garage door with Father Robert, we entered into a lovely and charming garden with a sweeping curve of stone boulders and other soft marbles of many colors that give a so, so soothing and an out-of-this-world kind of feeling. My hand was touching everything in sight, rubbing on this, feeling on that. I walked into the stately formality of a green rear garden, surrounded by boxwood hedges with low brick walls and jardinières in a bilaterally symmetrical composition that created a mirror image of the landscape. Going farther, the marbles turned into flagstone, reaching the bricks patio that are out of the view of the house. At the center was an open entrance to the gazebo and the pool. Standing there looking around, I thought I was pretty-boy Floyd's reincarnation in paradise on earth; and just when I thought my eyes had caught enough view, as we walked back to the house, there were more sight of the clay planter of beautiful bright marigold with little purple pansy blooming along the edge. Following Father Robert, he pulled out his keys from his pocket, fumbling the ring with his fingers. He let all the keys drop into the loop except the one he's holding with his index and thumb. He unlocked the sliding door, and we stepped into a splendid haven. I was afraid to set my foot on the superpolished wooden floor. It's so shiny that I could see myself in it. Then the round rug of many colors with a square mazelike design with white trim lying square in the center of the living room, reaching all the way to the front of the chimney that has white-colored tiles that connect the chimney to the hardwood floor. And there's the American flag standing on one side and the Oklahoma state flag on the other side. Above the fireplace a set of golden pots of azalea were on each side of a 30 x 24 wood-framed picture of Father Robert who looked like he's about to jump out at me with wire-rim glasses; on the same wall there's a life-size photo of Father Robert in his uniform, standing next to a tank, helicopter, and receiving an award for some brave act.

CHAPTER 3

On the wall were also the drawings of Michelangelo's *The Creation of Adam* and *The Temptation*. And there's the Frank Lloyd Wright lamp, a beige Norwalk leather lazy lounge chair. Along the wall was a bookshelf with an encyclopedia lined up in alphabetical order at the bottom. On the other side was the drawing of Giovanni Bellini, *The Annunciation*. The big screen, VCR digital light flashing, and stereo system with two twelve-inch speaker boxes on each side of the entertainment center. Going to the kitchen, in the center was an oak wood table the color of blood—with matching chair and decorated with a black-and-white checkered napkin. Yellowish green plate. All these are new to me. I take note of everything: the way the forks and spoon and knife are set pointing to the center of the table on top of the napkin. It's too much for me to take all of what I've seen in at one time. The dishwasher, chrome barstool, high ceiling light. Rack of spices. In the left corner was a lonely door that led to the other garden, this garden belonging to Kimberly, and she put a lot of love and care into beautifying it. Peeping out through the kitchen window, I saw my wife's lovely garden. She has a lot of roses, all kinds of colors, surrounding the water fountain that has an angel sitting on the edge, squirting out water. Kimberly looked up from what she was doing and asked her father, "Are you done showing him around, Father?"

"No, we're going upstairs right now," he responded softly and said, "Let's go," but I didn't hear him the first time he was speaking to me, and the second time got me to jump a little. Going up the Victorian brass-aluminum stairs, Father Robert showed me his study room and prayer room, which were pretty empty beside the black robe hanging that can be seen from the hallway in the open closet and a giant Bible sitting on top of the table, and the window was with white drapes. Before closing the door, Father Robert warned me that "this room is reserved only for prayer. A place to get close to angels and God." Across from it was his master bedroom, which he just pointed at with his finger and did not take me to see; moving along, we walked into another magnificent bedroom, which Father Robert told me, "This is my daughter's room," and he closed the door like he's afraid that I might see things that I'm not supposed to be seeing. Coming back down, Father Robert led me downstairs to a room, and that room has a bathroom next door to it. The room used to be a home office but was turned into my living quarters. I have my own everything: TV, radio, walk-in closet full of clothes, even a car would be given to me if I can get my license. Once we were done touring the house, we went to the kitchen where Kimberly was happily greeting us with the food that she had put together. The aroma of what she cooked smells different but good. She asked her father, "You finished showing Tommy around yet?"

"Yes! We went through the whole house," Father Robert answered. And he turned to me with, "So, how do you like your new home?"

"Like? This is heaven." But I tried not to show too much excitement, but it still showed anyway as the excitement was too much for me to conceal and was written all over my face.

CHAPTER 4

It was already dark by the time we were done with dinner. I watched a little of CNN with Father Robert while my wife cleaned things up, putting the pots and pans back in their place. I can't help but admire how she moved so gracefully and elegantly. I wanted to go help but was afraid of what Father Robert might have to say. So I waited for her to be done, and once she was, she came over and asked, "Father, are you done with Tommy? Because I want to take him up to my room."

"He's all yours, my daughter," the old man said.

Going up the stairs and across the hallway, I followed my wife behind like a dog in heat. Once the door closed behind us, inside her room, she asked, "So how do you like your father-in-law-to-be so far?"

And with my still-broken English, I said, "He's real nice, and you are very lucky to have a father like him."

Knowing it's true, she smiled proudly about what I said of her wonderful father and moved to pull me close, kissing me sweetly, only to break free, backing herself up to her bed, telling me, in a low tone, "I've never have a guy in my room before. You will be my first, and my last." Crawling onto the bed after her, thinking that I'm going to get some, I plan to make it last; but as I was throwing myself onto the bed, under my weights, the bed felt funny, like it had water in it or something. So I jumped back. That got Kimberly telling me, "What! It's a water bed." Then it hit her of where I came from; we don't have beds, especially one like this. Moving closer, I touched the bed again with amazement, then sat on it. But my wife got up and headed for the bathroom. I was like, "What the heck?" as I was ready to get it on; it's not the same as back in Cambodia, in the wild, where whenever we wanted to fuck, we just look around for a suitable spot, and we fuck dirty or clean, smelly or not. But here, I didn't know that we got to wash and clean our bodies up first, then the sex. She taught me a lot of other things, even manners and how to be polite and behave. She disappeared into the walk-in closet and came back out naked, making her way into the green- and white-tiled shower, and next to it was a low Japanese-style wall tub. Watching her showering and soaping her body down was like watching a movie. I loved the way she moved, so angel-like. I wanted to join her, but I held back my desire and turned to tweak on the water bed. "It's comfortable," I told myself. It's true; I never before laid my body or eyes on anything like this, and I was beginning to love it. She must take *hours* in the bathroom, or maybe it was because of the comfy bed that I fell asleep. Kimberly had to wake me up when she was done washing herself up.

"Hey! My husband, aren't you gonna wash up before we make love?" When I heard "wash up," I thought it was like the river, jump in and jump out and done; but when I got in the bathroom and saw the shower, I didn't see no water, and I don't know what to do to get the water to come out, so I just stood there, lost. Kimberly has to come and turn the water on for me, and she bathed me like a baby. Dried me up, she was ready to teach me sex education, as she started sucking on my cock.

CHAPTER 5

Pushing me onto the bed, she walked over to turn the light down low and press on the intercom to let her father know. "Father, we are calling it a night." And Father Robert just reminded her not to forget to pray. She prayed all right! On me, and like a cat, she's stocking ready to strike, taking my cock into her mouth, getting me harder than I'm already hard, before humming her choir on my balls. My wife was giving me the time of my life, and I was enjoying every bit of it, especially the way she was sucking on my brown-eye moaching, pulling everything inside out. She's a priest's daughter—like she can't confess all of her sins. Kimberly brought one of her legs and threw it across my body and went back to work on my cock again, exposing her pussy in my face for me to help her get out of hell and into heaven. Not really knowing what I'm supposed to be doing, I begin to lick, suck and mooch, finger fucking, and everything else, rubbing her clit and flickering and topping her lips. And with each new thing that I did to her, she only felt delight; the pleasures are paradise, a bliss for both of us. That night, we fucked long and hard, then slow and fast with little rest til morning. My wife showed me doggy style and let me fuck her in the butt hole, guiding me in and helping me out. I guess I shouldn't doubt the love she has for me. When we were both too exhausted to go on, we passed out in each other's arms. I woke up with Kimberly already working my cock. I opened my eyes to see a pair of titties bouncing in front of me. I was loving it. This was the life for me. I can live like this forever; but like all things that have been good for me, it didn't last, and this happiness also came to an end. At breakfast, I heard father and daughter's conversation. And my wife was going back to Southeast Asia. But I tried not to pay no mind. After we ate, both of them were dressed and ready to go somewhere. I was the only one still in my sleeping clothes. During breakfast, my wife told me, "Over here in America, everybody takes a shower every day. And tomorrow, that's the first thing you should take care of, your shower. Once you get in there, the first thing you do is brush your teeth, wash and shampoo your hair, scrub your body down with soap, rinse, and you're done." I was thinking, *Damn! Living in America has rules for everything.* Following close behind her, going back up the stairs, my wife took out her makeup box and went to sit at the end of the bed; she applied the makeup on her already-pretty face. And as she saw me just standing there, studying her, she ordered me to go hit the water. I did and with turning on and off the shower on my own. Stepping out, I dried myself and came out butt naked because I didn't have no clean clothes to wear. It's Sunday, and Kimberly's gonna dress me up herself. The clock read 6:40 AM, and she still has not finished with her makeup, her hair still wrapped in the towel into a bun on top of her head. As the waiting got longer and longer for her to be done so she can dress me up, I asked, "Can I go downstairs and get dressed?"

"No, because we have church today, and I want you to look good." Seven thirty, still I was waiting and butt naked. Another half hour gone by before my lovely wife finally finished. Putting everything away, she turned with a smile and asked, "How do I look?"

"Stunning," I told her with my dick bulging out the towel that wrapped around my nakedness.

I was ready to fuck again, but Kimberly tells me, "No! No! You're going to mess up my makeup, beside it's church." Coming back down, we went to my room, and she picked me out one of the blue suits that was already there for me before I got there. All tailor made. Once she finished dressing me up, inspecting me, she said, "There." I must admit I'm still pretty handsome, looking at myself in the mirror. My body was rock hard. You can say I'm all that. I smile at my other self in the mirror; I was proud of myself and glad that I took my time to work out in the darkness when I was a prisoner in Cambodia.

CHAPTER 6

It was 8:13 AM when we finally came out of the garage with Kimberly's 911 Porsche, a gray one, heading to the barber, because Kimberly didn't like the way that I looked. At 9:00 AM sharp, we were at the church after parking at the front of the entrance next to the steps that lead up into the church; we were being greeted and were meeting everyone. At 10:00 AM, the service began. I was introduced to the members of the congregation at the beginning of the service. After that, we prayed, "Amen!" And after the service, we went out for lunch, not to no fancy restaurant, but at Fort Seal, eating with the army. Kimberly is showing me off like Angelina Jolie showing off her Cambodian son to all the soldiers. We also went to a lot of other places for both shopping and recreation. I loved the way she drove or maybe the car, but I think it's the fact that I've never rode in a 911 before.

It was 4:15 PM when we got back home, and that was the last day that I'll share with her, as she has to go back to her mission in Asia and never return, not even her dead body when morning came. She was gone before I was awake; on cracking my eyes open and on knowing that she's not next to me when I awake, I cry because she's gone, and for myself. At least I'm grateful that she left me with the best fuck to remember. I got sad. I knew she's gone with only a note on the pillow. "I love you, wait for my letter," it read. And I waited and waited, but no letter came. Even though the sun was already up, for some reason, I still felt sleepy. So slowly I dragged myself along after reading the note, going to the bathroom to take a shower and take care of my hygiene as I was taught. Adjusting the water to a little over lukewarm, letting the sliding door fog before I stepped in and stood under the water, I missed how Kimberly used to bathe me like a baby. The hot water was so relaxing that I filled up the tub and soaked my body in. Resting my head on the back of the tub, I must've fallen asleep and woke up in cold water. I jumped up and out, pulled on the plug, turned the shower back on, and hopped back in, out again, dried up, and I got dressed, but I can't let go of the vision of my wife out of my head. My eyes were weak for her or for myself as I didn't know what to do. I wish I could go with her, and I still can't believe that she's gone. I didn't want to accept that another person was out of my life. Weakly climbing the stairs to go to her room to smell her scent, it's just how I remembered the same aroma since we first met. For the first time in my life I found myself praying, asking God, "Please, God, don't take the only good thing away from me." I have accepted enough bad to deserve this good and noble wife of mine. The cold breeze was coming in from the partly open window; I just sat at the end of Kimberly's bed. I didn't know what to do, and Father Robert won't be back for another five days as he's going on his missionary for Jesus. He showed me how to arm and unarm the alarm, and I was instructed to clean the church, and behind Jesus on the cross is where I hid my half of the key that I split with Chantho. From the time Father Robert left the house till his return, I ate Cocoa Puffs with Pepsi and watched wrestling until Father Robert's return. Seeing him pull up, I was happy. I rushed out to greet him, and he asked me, "How are you, my son?"

"Okay!" I told him, but inside, I was in disarray, and he knew it and was probably saying a silent prayer for me.

CHAPTER 7

That night we had dinner together, father and son-in-law, in complete silence. Also, it was the night that my workload was being added on for me to be responsible for. I now have to clean up the school that I'm attending with the small K-1 to K-6 children, and that's how I learned my English with the little children, but I quickly advanced. I was self-teaching myself, and Father Robert stepped in and showed me how to dream; I was reaching for the sky. But right when my hopes were high, the sad news came without any letter from my wife and on the TV tube, our last meal together; I'll never forget. The chef performing tricks, the fried ice cream, and the supermoist chocolate-mayo cake with blueberries sitting on top, a meal I will never forget, like the Lord's Last Supper. And in this town, everybody knows everybody. When Kimberly left, and when the news of her death came, they were all supportive and came to aid, comforting the father. I thought I had it hard, but Father Robert had it harder. Kimberly was his only child, and he was just beginning to enjoy her success, and like Job everything came crumbling down for Father Robert. It was all over the news. How the helicopter that my wife was in went wildly out of control and slammed into the mountain, sending smokes to the air. Watching the news over and over with Father Robert, he recorded the news. It was a sad case because she's such a beautiful and sweet cowgirl who believed in God and did good for others. After the news and TV goes off, Father Robert was having a serious talk with me; he said everything that belonged to me and Kimberly also belongs to me, but I didn't know anything about anything. I didn't even know what a stop sign meant so far. How was I supposed to know about the will? So I went on living my lonely life, doing my regular routine. Learning the moral of things and getting the taste of the work ethics and life in America. It's also a good thing that the bond between me and my wife was not yet established that strongly. So I was able to break off from her prettiness fast, but she never was out of my mind though. The memories of how Kimberly's helicopter went out of control and slammed against the side of the mountain with no survivor from a crew of twelve give me chills. Father Robert started to leave for out of town a lot, or maybe it was already his program before I got here. When he showed me home and taught me how to write checks and pay bills, he said, "You're gonna need to know the routine of living here in America. You have to be able to do this type of thing to survive." Most importantly he's a father to me. He's the one that taught me about life in general, giving me the wisdom and knowledge that I need to know on how to go about living. He wants me to inspire, to do my own things, mind my own business, leaving other people in peace, and taught me about lying. He stated that it's not good to lie whether with your mouth or on your back, and that hard work bring both health and wealth.

CHAPTER 8

I stayed in Kimberly's room a lot, to the point that Father Robert asked, "You like to take over the room? We can turn the one downstairs back to a guest and your study room." I agreed, and that's when my learning really began. "Here, here's a Bible for you, my son," Father Robert said, handing the Bible to me. "This book here is better than all the books put together, or ever written and I want you to read it, and continue to read it over and over again. I will bring you more literature, history of the greats so you can learn from the best." The first book was *The Art of War*—because Father Robert was an ex-navy—then autobiographies of Donald Trump, Steve Welch, President Nixon, Hitler, his commander Rommel and many more. I believe that Father Robert had big plans for my future. His vision might not be as big as to have me conquer the world, but to make a difference and creating a better living condition for myself and the people of the world that are less fortunate. Maybe my father saw in his dream that I am one of God's soldiers, one that will rise up someplace somewhere one day and make a difference. Or maybe it was just my imagination running wild, but whatever it was, it was with this room and from this house that transformed me into the man that I am today. Sometimes I wondered why my wife chose to leave her place here in America, which is considered to be a paradise on earth to third-world countries. There's nowhere else on earth like America, especially not in Southeast Asia. The difference is heaven and hell. Who can ask for more than living in a beautiful townhome, water faucet inside the house as well as bathroom and shower? There're people out there who don't even know what a sink looked like or have the food that are being thrown away here. Sometimes during my study, Kimberly would come into play, and I even got mad at her for trading luxury for oppression and death over life. I don't understand her. She already had a career here, but instead she chose to volunteer. And she did it with her all, even her own life. She didn't hold back nothing; I took a deep sighing to get air to my lungs and continued reading about the civil rights movement. The Black Panther and Huey Newton, and the people that received the Nobel Prize, only two presidents received this award, and now Vice President Al Gore for the global warming. My father taught me everything—the Western Billy the Kid, Jesse James to Bonnie and Clyde, the mobs, even the CIA to spy. He wanted me to be well versed all around. Knowledge and wisdom from the book of life, and intelligence and smartness from the best. And all this learning backfired on me when I moved to where there is my people in California because in Lawton, I never even run into one Khmer. It's like I was taken from one world and put in another like from my country to here in America.

Chapter 9

Father Robert had a nun, a professor in communication speech and human behavior. Her name was Sue Upchurch who came to the convent due to a series of bad relationships and marriage, one thing lead to another from bad to worse till she had enough of the world and decided to remove herself from it. But all that has changed as she found herself falling in love with me, and it happened in series. One thing led to another. Next thing we know we were doing our thang between teaching and study, fucking in between session using chair and desktop; the lust is there, but I have no feeling for this angel. Don't get me wrong though! She's beautiful and everything—slim body and long—everything down to her pussy lips the way it hang, but it's not enough for my brain. No matter what, I was still wrapped up with Chantho, the death of Mona and my stillborn, my wife Kimberly, and my own confusion and lonely life. So I just fucked for the hell of it, escaping reality for a moment. But it wasn't no fun and games for Sue when it came to her fucking. She pushed it over the limit and got us caught in the church bathroom by Father Robert. That day, he walked in, opened the stall, and saw Sue in the boys' bathroom on top of me who was sitting on the toilet, when he observed four legs sticking out. His heart must've popped and stopped breathing as he froze before he moved away without a word said. In my panic, I didn't know what to do. So I ran away. Once again, I was on my own, and even though I possess some knowledge about life, the odds are still stacked against me. I was by myself, and there's only one of me; and when you're by yourself, everywhere you go, you're gonna get broken. I slept in the yellow bus that was broken down and parked in the YMCA yard, eating the snack that I was able to fish out of the Sav-Way dumpster a lot of time; my thoughts turned to the first time that me and Sue began and relived the memory that I regret. I asked God, "Why me!" Why he has to save me from my death only for me to be tortured in hell while I'm still living? I want to know what's my sin, or what is it that I've done in my last life that I must suffer like a lonely vagabond flea.

CHAPTER 10

It started when Sister/Professor Sue Upchurch took off her glasses, and God she's prettier than I thought. Setting the glasses down, she told me to get up; as we were on the subject of self-confidence and present self, she said, "This is how you should move and position yourself straight and make sure your chest out." And it was like my hard body got electricity, it shocked Sister/Professor Sue Upchurch, the shock that got her saying, "Oh!" and started rubbing lustfully on my chest and, with her other hand, took hold of my dick and balls, taking it into her hand, and she squeezed on the nuts a little too hard that it almost crack my nut out of the sack that made me jump; she conceded, "You little bastard. You've been making me finger fucking and playing with myself, fantasizing about you from the moment I lay my eyes on you." Sue was a professor all right, as she guided me backward, bumping against the desk, swaying as we went, side to side; our concentration was not on where we're going but each other's body. Yes, her lust plus my fire together was all it takes. Sister Sue "hornily" pulled out my polo shirt tail out of my pants, the one that my wife bought me, and continued between clinched teeth, "You've been causing me too many sleepless nights, restless heart, and troubled soul, you have me thinking like a devil, and now I'm turning into one." And it started. The hard kiss on my neck and down to pull my pants down and had it hang at my ankle, Sue let her hot mouth work my already-hard cock. I got harder as I watched her in my head with my eyes closed, on how my dick goes inside her mouth. She's special, taking me all in, including both of my balls at the same time, or maybe I was just small. But for whatever reason, she seemed to like it in the butt and guided me inside her ass with both hands pulling her healthy cheeks apart. Once I was in like Mike Iron Tyson, I was jabbing, fucking the shit out of her swollen butt hole on top of my study desk. She was easy to maneuver around, or maybe she was just a professional. But whatever she was, she made me feel a different kind of love—one that was different from Chantho, Mona, and my wife Kimberly. Shaking the thoughts out of my head, I turned to think about my Chantho and jacked off to how I was gonna fuck her brain out, if I ever united with her and out of anger for abandoning me. I nutted and passed out with my pants hanging at the knees, leaning on the backseat of the toilet inside the YMCA bathroom. I woke up, couldn't believe myself, and I went back to my regular routine. I had found a place to recycle, so I collected cans for a living and made good money doing it.

CHAPTER 11

Everything went all wrong for me, even the seasons were against me. With only what I got on that Sunday, I was going to church and got caught with the weather; that night was cold, and the air didn't help as the chilly wind felt like it's ripping my face apart. My ears have become ice pops; moving slow with both hands in my pocket, I came to the row of parked buses and decided to take shelter. I found a sleeping bag in one of the buses, and I worked myself in and lay awake with the sleeping bag over my head, shaking. My mind tried to find a way out of this predicament, and a flood of sadness came over my heart, finding myself drowned in deep misery. I finally got some shut-eye and awakened hungry. Remembering the Sav-Way supermarket, my first thought was to go steal me something to eat. Circling the store, I tried to build enough courage to go inside and steal, but as I was coming to the back of the store my last time, I happened to see some workers throwing away the trash. So I waited till they're done and closed the roll-up garage door. Before I made my way to the dumpster, lifting the heavy plastic lid open, I climbed into the bin and began digging, not knowing what to expect. I found all kinds of food, fruits, and produce. I ripped open a bag of grapes and started to pop 'em by the handful. So every morning, I would take what food I found and take it to the park across town close to a high school, by the homemade lake. I would cook my food on the park grill using wood I gathered from the nearby woods. I was going around town like a vagabond flea, a lost puppy in a big city. I was going on the outskirts of the city when I discovered the recycling place. I started my can-picking career, mad at myself for throwing the good things away for a nut. But as I started to pick more and more cans, and the money was piling up, my greed stepped in; remembering the flea market that I have passed by so many times and saw the bike, I went and bought myself one, one that has a built-in carrier rack both in front and back. And with the business mind that I had, I was able to go back and forth from the recycling place faster than those who throw the can away to those that toss 'em out can consider them to be trash, but to me that was my bank: the more cans I bring in, the more money I made, and it happened. One night as I was coming home to the broken-down yellow bus with my load of cans, already ready for the recycling place to open the next morning, the sky up above was real dark, and the clouds were moving very rapidly. Luckily I wasn't too far from the yellow bus that I called home. The wind started to get stronger, making it almost impossible for me to move. All my cans were gone with the strong wind, and I have to abandon my bike, working hard and as fast as I can maneuver. I barely got to the bus and in time to turn and see my bike caught into the swirl of the wind, and the bus itself started to move into the air. Windows busted as it ascended off the ground. I crawled under one of the chairs and held on to the metal bars that were holding the seat in place. I must've gone twenty feet into the air before the bus landed on its side. Something must've poked at me on my side as it ached and ached bad. I took a break from my can picking after this and relocated in the summer close to the lake as I didn't want to bring attention to my winter hideout. Altogether, I had sixteen thousand cash in my possession, hiding it in shoes and belts. Coming to my regular bar dumpster that has been good to me, on jumping out with my can bag already thrown onto the ground, there's a drunk gay couple who happened to fuck close by. And on seeing me, a cute little Asian meat, for it I got beat up half to death; but I don't remember being sore around my butt ring as I try to felt for the aftermath pain while lying in the hospital, but no pain. They didn't take my money, and on the news it was said "a hate crime." Father Robert came to my aid; so did everyone else from the church.

CHAPTER 12

I was missing for three months. The police and Father Robert, including everyone else from the congregation, were searching for me. When I woke up in the hospital, Father Robert and Sue Upchurch, along with the police, were at my bedside. On seeing my father, I jumped, feeling the need to run. But I know I couldn't get away, so I brought my hand to cover my face as I was too embarrassed and ashamed to face my father with my disgrace, and it was like he understood. My father confronted me, "It's okay, Tommy, my son, I'm here to take you back home with me." On hearing this, I didn't know what to think or make out. Besides I've meant to be on my quest in searching for my Chantho; that's what my savings are for. I stayed in the hospital for a week—broken jaw, black eyes, and teeth missing—and there's not a day that Father Robert didn't visit me and talked promising words to me, telling me of his plan and the future goal he has for me. But when I came home, I only told him that I didn't want to join the service because of my past history with war, so Father Robert sent me to Alamo to be educated, where the head CEOs get their education, and I learned how to be a self-made. An academy that is known to produce entrepreneurs true to the school reputation. I've become one later on. But my schooling didn't last as I already knew most of the stuff already from being self-taught, and that's what I'm good at; besides, I understand that knowledge come from textbooks, and not the teacher nor the institution. On coming back to Lawton, it didn't feel the same and gave me no meaning to stay around. So after many days of contemplating, I made up my mind to go to where there is Khmer people in California, hoping to find Chantho. I told Father Robert about everything, and at the end, he said, "Well, my son, you have come a long way, and if you don't go now, your learning will not be of good use and you wouldn't be the somebody that you're distanced to be one day. But if you go, you are taking the responsibility out of my hand for me to help you but let me reassure you if you ever need me or a home to come to, the house and I will be here." Father Robert reassured me. There was sadness in his eyes and disappointment on his face as things didn't turn out as he had planned for me, but no matter what, I have to go. It's not about anyone, but myself, and I wanted to at least give love a try. I still have the half of the key, which is my hope. And the day before I boarded the Greyhound, I went and took the key from behind Jesus, where I had stashed it. Father Robert already had the ticket ready, and when it's time for me to depart, he handed me the ticket along with a $250,000 check, on top of my can-collecting fund. He also gave me a card to some type of business and told me that if I was ever in trouble, call the number on the card and ask for Mr. Cooper. At 11:00 AM of May 1, 1985, I got on the bus heading to Modesto, California—the town that I have come to call as home that has treated me so bad.

CHAPTER 13

The already-running bus was backing up, and through the window, I saw that Father Robert was crying; he removed the glasses from his eyes and dried his tears with his handkerchief. Sticky tears came down my cheeks as well; I didn't know if they were for Father Robert, my self, my *rest in peace* wife, someone, or something else. Coming through Oklahoma City, my first stop was Fort Worth, Texas. From there, I slept my way through El Paso. I got off there and en route on another bus heading to Los Cruces, New Mexico, and on to Tucson, cruising to Phoenix, Arizona; the Greyhound station was next to the airport station, and the plane can be seen ascending and descending in the clear sky. Coming out of the desert, I was refreshed at the new sight of Palm Springs. casinos, hotels, and lights brightened the city. People were everywhere, coming and going in and out of buildings like night creatures. After this excitement, I entered the miles of windmill of the desert. The Greyhound pulled over and went through the Indian Canyon. There's an insurance plaza with little hotel and apartment complex, and behind the busy street, that's where all the action took place. The hoes and pimps, drug dealers and users, buyers and traders conducted underground activity. San Bernardino was different. You get the view of the two mountains that were green with ice topping. It's a sight to remember. Going to Los Angeles, the station was hiding by the industry around it. The place was supercrowded that I almost got lost as I was hungry and went across the street to a taco truck that was serving more than just burritos, and it must be a regular routine for the cook to also ask to see if customers needed something else. And I told him no. And he responded, "No! Not food, I mean other stuff." I didn't know what stuff he was talking about, and I got kinda scared. So I didn't eat altogether, only what's in the machine. The forty-five-minute delay seemed forever as I'm in the long line waiting to go on northbound Interstate Five where there wasn't much to see. Besides it was already dark. When I got to the

Lancaster station, there wasn't any passenger to pick up, so we just emerged to 99 and cruise into Bakersfield through Fresno, Madera, Merced, and finally my final destination Modesto, California—the city that I came to love and treated me so bad. Where I found love and lost my freedom, my wife, my children, and everything else I have.

CHAPTER 14

I arrive at the Modesto old Greyhound bus station on Eleventh Street. At the time the population was 105,000, and the whole town was under heavy construction. Builders put up houses like crazy, as people from the Bay area came flooding to buy cheap houses in exchange for commuting. I myself was new to the town, so I started to ask around to see if there were Cambodian people residing anywhere in town. The Mexican lady that I spoke to told me, "Oh yes! They even got a Cambodian town. It's on the west side of town on Paradise Road, 620 Paradise."

I asked, "How do I get there?" So she pointed to G Street and told me to just go all the way straight until I hit the old New Deal and the bank then the apartment complex. Right behind it.

"You can't miss it," she said. True to her word, I didn't have no problem finding 620 Paradise alone and without parents and no guardian of any type; I found myself quickly in the wrong things, with the wrong crowd, and troubles caught up to me real quick. With the money that I have, I started to live the life of the prodigal son. I got myself a two-bedroom upstairs apartment, and the party began. Me and some friends and young peers both from junior and high school, we all hang out. For the Asian, going to school during the '80s was to live a double life. A straight-A student on paper and a good child at home but at the same time gangbang between classes and after school at the park and in alleyway, but what the world perceived as "one of the most notorious Asian gang in American history," only if society knew. Modesto Hit Squad was based on liberty and justice. We're just soldiers of a freedom fighter like the civil rights movement, and without a leader, who has a dream? We were a bunch of immigration kids whose parents didn't speak a lick of English and only had each other to lean on, so we stuck together and earned our spot in equal treatment and rights. And like everything else, the peace we fought for also came with a price. And along the way, straight As get a life-without-parole sentence, and much thanks goes to M! Along with the bunch, I got caught up with a gun charge and got sent to CYA (California Youth Authority), with an M number; even though the Hit Squad are scattered all over the place and locked away throughout the state, as a whole, we are one. Together we had a plan for all of us to escape poverty, and as one, we will do our best to turn every member's dream into reality. It's gonna take hard work, and everybody has to get their part done or will do their part; and in ten years, the plan was to come back together and to start the Modesto Hit Squad anew, one that'll be more corporate—this time, coming together with knowledge, skills, abilities, and most important of all, *money* to rebuild the foundation. But so far, it turned out not according to plan. Everybody was dropping out and ditching school to go hang out at the river, smoking, drinking, hitting the bamboo bong. The whole organization was falling apart before anything even started; one by one, we're being picked up by the pigs that came down hard on the Asians. While I was locked up, Father Robert flew all the way from Lawton to visit me for a couple of hours in Stockton Youth Authority along with his accountant/lawyer, Mr. Cooper, for me to sign some legal paperwork using another inmate's visitor as witness to the signing of the paperwork that I cared little to know for what or ask questions about.

CHAPTER 15

After serving my YA sentence, when I got released two and a half years later, I didn't bother to call my father. Once I touched down, I was too ashamed to face him as I have nothing to show for. I got involved with a girl—white one—and forgot about my quest for Chantho as I found myself in love. Sina was all right, but she's not Chantho. It didn't take me long to get tired of her and get violated; once I sit in jail, Sina was nowhere to be found—out of sight, out of mind. My father again flew down from Lawton to spend a couple of hours with me on a weekend visit; one thing that he did, he always encouraged me to keep on learning, keep on reading the Bible, and to look at my predicament the same way as I was going to an all-boys' school. So I took his advice and dedicated nights and days, weekends, and holidays—no break, no vacation—strictly educating myself. But not every inmate agreed with me, and it happened as I was at the NRCC (Northern Receiving Center for California) in Sacramento. We were in line going to chow, and chaos broke out everywhere; everybody scattered all over the institution, out in the open fields as well as the kitchen and living quarters. The alarm was going off, and staffs came running from all direction with pepper spray in their hands, some with beanbag guns. I was in line holding my tray, next in line to get my food served to me. One of the football-size players came charging at me like I had the ball. I was already lost to the action surrounding me. Thinking fast, eyes big watching him coming at me like a bull, I moved to my left with my tray; and as a bullfighter, I let him have it with the metal tray when I turn back around, cracking the back of his head open, only to catch a punch from I don't know whom. I got knocked-the-fuck out and woke up in the MTA (Medical Treatment Administrative). The nurse told me that I got hit by a battery pack, eight stitches on my right eye; from here I was sent to the Segregated Housing Unit (SHU) where I did most of my studies in a hole on a 23-1 lockdown, twenty-three hours lockdown and one hour of recreation time in a boxer and a T-shirt. Sacramento hall had a reception and orientation area on one side, and the other side are the holes you don't get to have nothing, and I have 120 days of hole time. After a week, I was bored out of my brain; I asked one of the staff for a Bible. And he was religious enough to provide me with one. And again I read the Bible over and over til I was out of confinement. I managed to parole without more time added to my sentence.

CHAPTER 16

During the time I was stuck in confinement, having time to myself, I made plans, but my dedication wasn't there to stick to it. And as soon as I got free, I didn't waste no time in getting back to the bed I once slept on. I got my own place again and started to hang out with the homies. Fresh out, I needed a fresh fit and fresh everything else including a piece of meat to beat on. Me and a couple of the Hit Squad headed for the mall, and I was checking everything out—fat one, skinny one, pretty one, ugly one, they all are beautiful. All of them looked good to me; and as I was glued to this fine slim blonde to the far side of the mall and I saw her, my heart wanted to believe it was Chantho just as I remembered, but I told myself it can't be. And by now I learned not to let anything be the reason to stop me short, so I walked over; my eyes always gave to her, but I acted like I was checking out some rings in the glass showcase inside the jewelry store. I tried to get a real good look at her to double-check my eyes, to be sure that it's Chantho. And my heart jumped at the smile that I remembered as she was talking to the salesclerk. It has to be her because there's not another smile like hers. I approached her with the norm and gave her my number without revealing myself. It didn't take long for me to get to know her name, and it turned out not to be my beloved Chantho that I lost. Since it's not my lost love, I never brought my past up with Sara Long, but how she told me the story about her life; I wanted to ask her about Athom, if she knew Athom, but my tongue just rolled up. Sara Long said that she was lucky that her husband brought her out of the killing field. When she first arrived in America, she landed in San Francisco and lived there till she and her husband had a child and decided to move to somewhere a little slower to raise their children—a daughter, named Elisabeth. If it wasn't for the key that was around her neck, I would never have found out that her mother was my lover of old. She has changed her name from Chantho to Sara, taking up her husband's last name, Long. We were so crazy in love all over again once we discovered the truth about one another, but there were a couple of things that were in our way of happiness and everything good together. For Sara Long, it was her husband, and for me the parole and the authority. I was already running from the law at the time, and when I told Sara Long about it, she wanted to run away with me; she even came up with a solution for us. She has a half sister who lived in the East Coast (Lowell, Massachusetts), and we could run away to there. Not wanting to do time and with my desire burning to be with Sara Long, I agreed to go with her plan, leaving Elisabeth behind with the grandparents. With a pound of weed for the trip, we boarded the Greyhound, the two of us on the move. Sara Long paid for everything as she thought that I was just one of those Modesto Hit Squad no-good-for-nothings that don't have a penny to my name. Only if she knew the things that I didn't tell her about me; my self didn't know the half of it. I really didn't know what I have by now. I understand about those who think they have something when they don't have nothing, and those that don't say they got anything have everything; besides, I don't want to assume.

CHAPTER 17

On Friday, January of 1985, our love on the run began. We started out with one suitcase apiece; and inside of my case was my pound of weed and in Sara Long's, a .22 Jennings for safety and protection purposes, because we're heading to a place that we didn't know nothing about, so better safe than sorry. The Greyhound door slid close, and the driver let the air brake go; the bus started to slowly back up, moving slow enough for all the departing to wave good-byes to family and friends—in our case, Elisabeth and the grandparents. The bus pulled out from the lots and made a left turn on K Street, right on Sixth Street, and right onto 99 North Freeway when the light turned green to give the right of way. The Hound came to a full speed. I turned to take Sara Long into my arms, held her tight as we're passing familiar sights. The trip was exciting for both of us; and we were too much into each other, busying ourselves with kisses, touching, rubbing, and feeling on each other that we didn't notice we had passed the little town and places that we used to know and go visit and take on trips too. We stopped smacking our lips when we got to Galt and held one another's hands into the Sacramento station to transfer to a bus that would route us to our next destination. My heart was pounding, as I stepped out of the bus, and my eyes were everywhere with the pound of weed and Sara's .22. I was scared half to death, looking around for cops, but I didn't spot no lawmen in sight; still we didn't sit around and wait neither. We quickly got out of the bus and waited to be the last one to pick up our luggage because I was afraid that they might have dogs, but so far so good; and we boarded the scheduled bus without interference, showing the short black man our tickets. He looked at it and handed it back to Sara. We went to take our seats at the same spot at the back of the bus, and we got going again. The bus rolled around a couple of blocks and entered Freeway 80 that took us to Reno, Nevada, and from the depressing snow; it got me feeling sad, but it was a great blessing, the sight of the city light and its beauty. From a distance we can see Circus Circus and Marriott; as we passed, I kind of wished we had a chance to enjoy the Sin City. Getting a taste of the never-asleep and forever-up city, checking out the people to see how they lived, and playing their card game or slot machine, at that instance, I imagined I had Sara Long next to me, cheering me up as I hit the jackpot. Only to come back to what I want, to just pass on by; I watched people from the Hound moving around, going and coming, in and out of building. When I turned to look back, I saw the MGM and the Hilton Hotel standing tall and proud. Going, the bus gave one last sound and picked up speed. I blew a kiss to say good-bye to the desert oasis and slowly moved northeast to swing by Winnemucca Elko, picking up a package. Sara was asleep on my shoulder as I was rocking away to Groove Theory; it helped me steal a chance to let my mind ponder a little on my plan, my future, the outcome of my life, and the aftermath. But I found it hard to listen to music and try to think at the same time, so I silenced the sound. And before I could come up with anything, I, too, was sound asleep with a new hope and a smile on my face. Waking up again only to find Sara still asleep, watching her evenly breathing, I moved my hand to disturb her sleep with a kiss on her forehead, and I played with her hair. Her tits didn't seem or feel any bigger from when we were back in the Cambodian jungle. Or maybe she lost it all after she had Elisabeth, because I saw some of her photos that showed boobs. Besides, I was too much in love to worry or ask her about anything stupid as to what happened to her. I was enjoying myself playing with her pussy and lost in my own world of fantasy that I didn't see the little white boy watching me. When we locked eyes, he rubbed his fingers as though to say "shame on you."

CHAPTER 18

After the death of my wife (Kimberly), and a couple of worthless-than-pieces-of-shit hoes that came into my life, I thought I couldn't bring myself to love another soul, but this is not just an ordinary female dog. She's my Chantho, my lover of old; she's different from the rest. I leaned closer to her and whispered into her ear, "I love you, Sara Long"; but as I remembered the vows that we took under oath at the temple back in Cambodia, swearing in front of God and the angels that til death we'll never be apart, hell not even death are strong enough for love, for some reason I cannot seem to be able to bring myself to forgive her for abandoning me when I'm still alive, and in the time when I needed her most. But like always, love conquers all. I leaned over and kissed her again on the forehead, awakened her as we pulled into some small town where a passenger was getting off. Coming out of Nevada, we pulled out the bread and tuna. We had tuna sandwich, and after we had our fill, we turned to enjoy Sara's favorite tune—TKA's "Louder Than Love"—the headphone tickling our eardrums. We listened to it over and over again. With the road deserted late in the night, without too much traffic, with no stop to make, the bus driver let the pedal hit the metal and smashed our way till we reached Salt Lake, Utah. From the bus station, we could see the Delta Center, home of the Utah Jazz. Back on the highway, going across the state, we passed fields and fields of saltwater and pulled over into Rockspring. We stopped for food, stretched out, used the restroom, and smoked. I smoked all right, my weed. I killed the joint and had my eyes real low, with a smile on my face by the time we got back on the Hound. I was a distance away from all the passengers in the snow, as I didn't want no one to smell the weed aroma. I doubt it that it did any help as the buds were superstankin'. I was coughing my lungs out, pounding on my chest with a closed fist, and a snowball hit me on my back. I was like, "What the fuck!" So I turned to look, and it was only my Sara playing with me, smiling. Telling me that "the stuff gonna kill you." And she threw a couple more snowballs at me as I came charging to take her in my arms. I knocked her down to fall onto the snow. Lying there, Sara made herself a snow angel and ordered me to do one next to her. I was about to lie down when she sprang up, laughing, and threw more snowballs at me. We were two grown kids playing, and I chose to lose, took off running, while Sara was right behind me. I turned and caught her into my arms, picked her up off the ground, and spun her around. I kissed her long like her last name, and I wanted to make it last forever. I let her down, and together hand in hand, we're headed for the restaurant because I had the munchies. We had burgers and fries. We were the first two to be back on the Hound. I was all tight eyes and smiling. We took turns feeding each other, giggling, and laughing like two little boy and girl on a school bus. People were watching us, but we didn't give a shit because they aren't gonna give us a dollar; so we kept doing our thang till we fell asleep with our Walkman still on and awakened to "Louder Than Love" booming in our ears.

CHAPTER 19

We were awakened when the bus slowed down to enter Laramie, a little town—too small to be even considered as one—about five houses, and that's the whole town; I imagine, everybody knows everybody, even the dogs' names, but it's surrounded by a homemade lake with ducks swimming, and a camping ground. Next was Cheyenne, also a lonely small out-of-nowhere, depressing place that got Sara feeling sad. Not about her husband, her daughter, or herself, but about the time when she abandoned me, leaving me to face the world alone while she got saved by her hero Sean Long, an American soldier. She knew she had broken her promise, and for that, she planned to make it up to me by committing herself to my world. Looking out the window, Sara saw my reflection studying her, which got her even sadder as she saw the hurt that still lingered in my face just as she had last saw me. And to even my emotion out, she reached over and rubbed my face with her thumb as her palm cupped around my face. She smiled, but there were tears in her eyes. She took a couple of deep sighs, and she reassured herself, *I'm gonna love him like he has never been loved before.* Still smiling to her own satisfying result, she turned and planted a gentle kiss on my cheek. Going through Kearney and out of Wyoming, we went past Grand Island and slept our way to Lincoln, awakened long enough to only take the headphone off our ears, and slept some more out of what's left of Nebraska and roll into Omaha at the break of dawn. We came to Des Moines and stopped again for food—but for me, to smoke some more weed. That humble baby green weren't no joke, choking the life out of me and getting me superstoned out of my head. I was eating up everything; my thoughts drifted to Sue Upchurch, and I quickly shook her out of my mind. I can't believe, Sue Upchurch, of all people. Moving out of Iowa City, we inched along the stretch of Interstate 80 to catch a view of Deanport. I had enough of this bus ride, and I'm too tired to pay attention to anything. So I closed my eye to try and catch some Zs. But sleep can't find my eyes, so I let my eyes explore as we went.

CHAPTER 20

Days turned into night, and the snow were getting thicker by the miles. The trees and fields are blanketed with white. The wind in the air also seemed to pick up a little. We've been on the Hound for two days and two nights, and so far, I didn't like it. I was so exhausted that I didn't realize we were in Illinois or the stop at Moline. Sara told me that we're at the Chicago station, picking up a couple of single travelers, and we headed out to leave the windy city behind. No wonder I noticed the wind picking up. A package was being dropped off at Gary without any pickup, and the Hound came to a stop at South Bend in front of McDonald's. It was here in the bathroom that Sara Long ever committed a public act. She was already inside the McDonald's supposedly ordering for us while I went to smoke some more weed. Eyes low, smiling, all high, bumping my head against the cloud, entering the cozy restaurant, I approached Sara, sitting at the table with the food already ordered; on seeing me, her smile brightened up as lust took over desire. And when I got to where she sat, she quietly told me, "I got an idea!"

I said, "What?" "Let's go in the bathroom." She giggled. I looked around; as I've got the idea and with the desire to fuck her brains out like I have planned long ago for what she has done, leaving me to be alone and all, I sneaked into the girls' bathroom after her. It was awkward because this was new to both of us, but we managed to work the toilet. Only if we fuck a minute longer, we would be stuck in Indiana. I didn't think it was that long that we're fucking, but I guess when you're feeling good, you lose track of time. We didn't even had the chance to grab our food off the tables as we saw the McDonald's empty of passengers, and the bus was about to move out when we came running out of the McDonald's. That we will never gonna forget as long as we live. It's a good thing we didn't miss the bus, or else we'd be stuck in the middle of nowhere; plus I was on the run too, and that would suck.

Chapter 21

Exhausted from the hard fuck and the short sprint, I was surprised that Sara still had a brain to function. I didn't know that we had gotten to Toledo; what a depressing mile and pile of snow sight. Sara was looking sad; she was thinking about something, maybe about Elisabeth. She cried and refused my comfort all the way till we're out of Landusky. Then she fell asleep; I followed right behind her like how I nut after her orgasm. Waking up together, we were in Cleveland. Here we had a six-hour delay waiting for the changeover or the snow to be kind enough to make way. So with the delay, we decided to lock our luggage up in the coin-operated locker and take a tour of the city. The people here were interesting. Nice and friendly, easygoing, making me think about the people back in Lawton, Oklahoma, even when they're cold, they still took their time to say hi and hello or a nod of the head! I even ran into a real hillbilly, the whole nine yards. The guy has the hat, the beard, the farmer suit, and the girl in her blow-up dress looked so adorable. I admired her a little too long, and my passion wondered what's under the dress and what her pussy looked like and what color—crazy me. I shook the sick thought out of my head and walked over to get up close and personal, and they told me, "This is our first time that we met anyone from Cambodia," as I admit that they're the first real hillbilly we met in person. Bidding them goodbye, I took Sara's hand and headed out the station only to look for a place to smoke my weed, and a place to eat was our intention, but it turned out we ended up in the Cleveland Inn. It was here that Sara, for the first time, tried 69s and into her butt to see what kind of ecstasy it would bring. I think she was lying as she gagged and choked, but whether in truth or pretend, she was sucking; we guided each other slowly through. When I tried to put my dick in her butt though, Sara said, "It hurts, it hurts."

"Shhh! It's okay, baby," I comforted her, rubbing her back and her cheek while cracking her bottom cheeks open at the same time.

"Uuw! No! No!" she begged but only got me bent lower from behind, and I kissed the back of her neck, rubbing her side, staying put as to soothe the inching pain that I forced myself in. Goddamn, her asshole was heaven, and I was fucking an angel because I never experienced anything like her asshole before. We hopped in the shower after the stinky and painful fuck that made me want to puke from the smell. Tiredly we made our way back to the Hound station, forgetting to even to eat, and in that below-zero-degree weather, it didn't help; even with the well-prepared clothing that Sara did, I'm still freezing my balls off because I'm not used to the cold and never wants to get used to it neither.

CHAPTER 22

In Ohio, it gets dark fast, and the bus didn't pull up till 7:00 PM. We still got an hour to wait, so I went outside to kill the time by smoking some more weed, get my eyes low, and put a smile on my face. Coming back into the station high, I walked on air to get to where Sara sat waiting, listening to music, and I joined her. But that, too, didn't cure my boredom. So I went to the arcade and must've wasted a ton of quarters. By the time I was done, people started to fill up the waiting area, and all at once, buses for all different routes came rolling in. Everyone was in a hurry to get on their destination buses because the cold was unbearable. Inside, the bus was warm and cozy, but the seat was getting real uncomfortable for my ass. And as we went, we were able to catch a little sight of what's left of Pennsylvania; the driver made a quick stop in Eric. And by morning time, we entered New York, stopping in Buffalo, the coldest lower part of the United States. We got a glimpse of the majestic Niagara Falls; and even though it's early morning and the fog still hang in the air, there were people and tourists already all over the park—some with camera, others just sightseeing. I liked the view of the wide waterfalls. I tried to look for the wonder and the mystery behind the falls, but all I saw at the bottom was white smoke mixed with the cloud that I was blowing before I boarded the bus again. From here to Rochester, Schenectady, and Albany, the Hound kept going, missing no parts of New York. Moving from I-80, we merged into I-90, and the next stop was Worcester onto Boston, and we took Route Three to reach Lowell, which is about another half-hour ride. Massachusetts was different than all other places across the United States. Even their language is strange. They still smoke in public places. Old folks still gather in the donut shop, enjoying coffee and donuts, having a good time, chitchat talking about the weather and the news of the day, Bob and Jay. But for the most part, it's quiet with everyone going on with their business and praising their Celtics, especially now that they are championship contenders again with their star Larry Bird at the time. The lives are rich and full of celebration, getting drunk, going to and from places to places, talking about the future of the Celtics and their own and how it's like after retirement, and so on.

Chapter 23

When we arrived at Boston, Sara had placed a call to her sister and her sister's husband along with their daughter, who were already waiting for us at the Lowell station that we didn't notice. The sister, whose name was Bim, when she saw us get off the bus, she was on her husband's lap, who was tired from his job and was trying to get some shut-eye. She ordered her husband, "Honey! They're here, go help 'em take the luggage, they're tired from the long trip."

He slowly got up and obeyed. And once he took the luggage, my baby green weed aroma hit his nose, and the smell was so strong that it got him. "Man! What's that smell?"

"What?" Bim responded.

And he repeated, "You didn't smell it?"

"Smell what?" she said. On hearing what they talked about, me and Sara just looked at each other with blank faces.

But Sara with her quick wit stepped in and saved the day, coming up with an explanation, "Oh, it's throw-up clothing in there. We got bus sick." So the husband backed off and tossed the suitcase in the little rumbling trunk of a four-door Corolla; and when all of us got in, it was scraping the pavement, but the little machine kept chucking. We were the only Asians on the Hound, so it was easy for Sara's half sister to spot us. The sister was pretty looking, the husband looked pretty tore up, and they have an adolescent daughter who was beginning to grow into a woman, with her figure taking curves, real bright eyes, and a shiny smile. She's gonna grow up and knock a lot of motherfuckers out. Sara and her sister haven't seen each other since their separation during the war. The brother-in-law's name was Lou; and he's a tight-eyes, tight-ass motherfucker, squeezing every penny and working his hardworking ass off, holding two jobs, getting paid $22 an hour at one job and $16 the other, and he still ride a bike to work and to get around town. Their house was about fifteen blocks away from the station, on Lawrence Street right next to a small river, and across the street was an old red brick building, which the agency lease as their office; the temp staff there helped me and Sara land a job at a plastic factory producing laundry baskets and tubs. The house was built in the '50s and looked pretty beat-up, with a cracked-paint front porch that was badly in need of a new paint; it has three steps leading up to the front door. The first floor of the house was half living room, half kitchen and dining and divided by the bathroom and shower and then the kitchen with a door that led down to the basement. Upstairs was two small bedrooms and a bathroom, and one of the room was ours, overlooking downtown. I thought that the family would want to be close to each other and share the same floor and room next to each other, but no, we have to get one of the upstairs bedrooms. Looking out of the window, I could see the little stream moving forever gently and gracefully with the billboard on top that read "American run on Duncan." A karate class was taught down the street in a much-older building. Going uphill, there's an unused train track, and across it was a gas station and a massive field of burial ground. In the middle of the "rest in peace" is a road that took lead to the shopping plaza, and there's a Baily fitness center that I join. I often used this gym as my personal office where I conducted my affairs of my underworld life that I kept secret from Sara Long. My mission was clear: to find me an outta-state girl on the side and find an easy opportunity to make a living. From the Olympic-size pool, to the fly machine, the bench press, steam room, and locker room are where I'm talking to new, different undercover people and girls who I'm trying to get to know; I met 'em all here. My underground activities are done here in secret and without notice, except from Sara Long.

Chapter 24

It's been two and a half months; and so far, I have ran into two persons, and everything else seems gloomy, making me feel depressed and sad at times. And if it wasn't for the pound of weed I brought along with us, I'd probably be back in Modesto that same day we've arrived, but the weed kept me going—every day from morning till 4:00 PM, and 4:00 PM to whenever I come home. Everywhere I go, I would look around, open my eyes and ears to any given opportunity for a chance for me to make easy money both legal and illegal; I don't care as long as I don't have to work. I use the excuse of my going to the gym, answering Sara with the question, "You don't want your man to look all sucked up, do you?" I would always throw this line in her face whenever I can't get out of something or needed an excuse to meet someone at the gym. On the morning that I was running late, as I didn't want to get up and go bust my ass making plastic baskets and tubs, I was happy the lady that was carpooling with us was also running late; and the elder woman forgot her lunch pail, so coming out with it was her daughter, and her name is Sammie—your mother, Diamond and Cryxtal. Yes! She was young, and she fell in love, and out of all people she chose me. I didn't take notice at first, because she was still in adolescence; besides, me and her brother Map, a mechanic by trade whom I met while working out, have a money-making idea, but not enough capital to start our talking business-building rapport. After we got to the talking and sharing opinions, I saw a perfect opportunity to make easy money. So I called up Mr. Cooper. Pulling out the card for the first time since Father Robert had handed it to me, using the pay phone, I dialed the number, and the phone rang on the other end; a lady picked it up. "Good afternoon, Anderson and Cooper. This is Linda, how can I help you?"

"Yes! I like to speak with Mr. Cooper?" I requested.

"He's in a conference at the moment." And she offered, "Can I take a message, and have him call you back?"

"No!" I told her. "I'm calling from a payphone, and if I can just bother you to interrupt the meeting and tell him my name I would greatly appreciate it."

"And what is your name, sir?" she asked.

"Tommy! Tommy Ok."

I was put on hold to hear another lady's voice telling the history of Anderson and Cooper. The history was cut short as Mr. Cooper's voice boomed in my ear, "Tommy!"

"Yes! It's me, Mr. Cooper, and I'm sorry to disturb you with your conference, but right now I need a small favor from you." I told him of my new resident; he asked me about my parole situation, but I cut him short with my new and exciting opportunity, asking him to get me all the information about the standing car auctions to be sent to me. I requested both local and state including federal auction in the Massachusetts State and/or at least within two hundred miles.

"Well! Tommy, you really surprise me with your request, and I'll have that out to you ASAP," Mr. Cooper reassured me. "And hey! Listen. The conference is still going. I'll get that out to you, but I gotta run, give the address to my secretary. Better yet lay the detail out for her because she's the one who will be assigned to do the research to your request."

"What are you planning to get in to?" Linda the secretary asked once she's back on line. I told her that I'm planning to open and start a used-car lot. "Where would you like your resource to be sent to?" And I told her the address, 107th St. Lowell, Massachusetts.

"No phone," I told her. "I'll call, when I receive the information that you will send me." We bid our good-byes, leaving me anxious as I hang up. I was really looking forward to the possibility.

Chapter 25

The package arrived fairly quick; and as soon as Map told me that my mail has arrived, the next day I played sick, and I didn't catch the van poll with Sara to go to work. As soon as the van turned the corner, I was out the front door, heading to Map's house to check my mail. I had on hooded sweats and a jacket over my wifebeater on. I was sweating dog and duck as I was jogging my way to Map's house; when I got there, I have to take my jacket off. Once I was inside the house, and it happened before I even had a chance to rip the envelope open that was in my hand, coming out was Sammie. She was on her way out to school. She is such a model—tall, very beautiful, and a knock-out form. Big ass, tits, and butt like one of those rap guy Snoop Dogg's "girlfriends." My eyes were pleased with what I saw, but Sammie was more pleased as she liked what she was seeing, and her eyes drove her heart to desire to have me as her future husband; I guess all the working out that got my body rock hard really turned her on. But then again that's what comes from working, "health and wealth." Sammie kept all of her passion off to herself till the time came. Map has to encourage me to open the package as my eyes were beholding her beauty. Ripping the envelope open, there were all sources of information used on car auctions; and there's a note from Mr. Cooper, explaining about the salt factor and how I would lose money if I don't find buyers fast enough to purchase the already-used cars that sits with salt clinging to it. Mr. Cooper said, "A value of a car going down versus the appreciation of the house. Both are not the same. Car value go down every day, and the value of real estate goes up every day." And Mr. Cooper advised me from going into disaster, and with this clear understanding of things, I told Map that I'm sorry and explained to him how the business is not gonna be successful. I even tried to make him see things with different eyes, that things are not as good as it looks sometimes, because what you see and what you hear are not the same as what you know, and his reply was, "It's all right. I want to give my ability a try anyway." But I knew that it's not okay; I saw there was disappointment in his eyes and on his face. I didn't want to make matters worse, so I didn't say anything in response and turned my attention back to Sammie, who was in the kitchen checking me out the whole time even though she was running late for school. I told myself, yeah, she's beautiful, but only in a dream, I'll be with someone like her; besides, she's still an adolescent, and I'm already in my midtwenties and have a relationship. But Sammie was determined and had a lot of patience to go with it, because even after I was gone, she came looking for me.

CHAPTER 26

The temp agency has to send me to another factory, because I wasn't getting along with the hard work, and someone was using his hand to think for himself as floor supervisor. Now I'm working for Thompo's and bits in Orange. Making plastic ties, at the same time my underworld activities are getting to be too much for me to handle. I found it hard trying to run a gambling shack, being a dope man, and running other operations such as finding the right girl for the prostitution. My cover-ups are limited, and the games are starting to catch up on me. Sara started to suspect there's something that's going on that she does not know about and needs to find out. She started to go through my personal belongings, coming close to pinning me down. When a book of matches was found in my pocket that read "call me," problems arise at the house. The brother didn't like the way I take care of my business and how I'm living, trying to tell me what to do because I lived under his roof, talking to me like I'm his son; and when I didn't give in, he labeled me as a loser, so I got mad and told him, "Fuck you, punk!" and with that I got both of us kicked out. Sara beforehand knew that I done fucked up. She started packing, only to toss both of our suitcases on the porch, and together we took off walking in the snow; not used to it, Sara and I almost got frozen. There was no place to go, so we made our way to the Baily fitness center; and once inside, we took comfort of the heat of the gym. It seemed to be the end of the road for us; it was time for us to call it quits and catch a plane back home to California, but no, I have to run into the white cat that I was working with at the warehouse. He happened to have a membership at Baily fitness and showed up right before we were out the door, to go look for a Western Union so the grandparents can wire us some plane-ticket money.

"Hey Bob! What you doing here," I sparked the conversation, extending my hand for a handshake. "You come here regularly?" I asked.

"This has been my gym for five years now," he replied. Looking at him though, and calculating the time he's been working out, the gyms are doing him no good, because the belly is bigger than the cag itself. As I was about to push the double glass door open to leave, he asked, "Are you done?"

"Yeah!" I sadly lied. "Besides, I didn't come here to work out today."

So he proceeded, "Then what are you doing here?" So I told him what had taken place at home to get us kicked out.

"I don't have a place to go."

"Well, my aunt owns apartment complexes on Third Street on the other side of the river, and If you like, I can talk to her for you," Bob offered, and I more than gladly accepted.

CHAPTER 27

With each passing day, Sara's feelings grew more and more insecure, and her thinking brought her mind's eye to see stupid things like, "Your bitch from Stockton come looking for you. She would assume and accuse, that's why you have to make time for her. She would come up with finding someone new, that's why we didn't fuck like we used to, but I haven't changed, still pushing and running my basement small-time operation. Finally, I came home one night after going to the dance with Sammie for the first time. We kicked it off smooth and quickly became good friends, but what freaked me out was what she told me: "One day I'm gonna marry you, and make you my husband." I'm thinking, she's trying to send me to prison, and I have to get away from her before something happens. It's only been a month at the apartment that Bob helped us get in, and Sara was ready to go; besides, she really, really misses her baby. So I was able to persuade her to catch a flight home first, while I stayed back with my little small-time dope game, at the same time hiding from Sammie; she was hawking me down from the sky. I run and run, and I hide and hide here and there, but Sammie and her mother's beat-up old Buick kept catching up to me till the authority set in and fucked up my $100,000 invested—a loss that was hard to accept, but I swallowed hard, accepted the loss, and got myself ready to go back home, or try again somewhere else. So I sold the remaining of my avenue, from selling stolen goods to electronics, chopping cars, and all that other shit, but like I have said, "I was alone, and when you're by yourself, anywhere you go you will get broken." I called up Sara Long, who was already in Modesto at the grandparents' house, and told her, "You don't need to wire me no money." It happened that on the same day, the same temp agency found me another company to work for. She was happy and sad, and mad when she heard the announcement of my plan of going to Detroit with my underworld operation that came crumbling down on my head, which

I didn't reveal to her. I made up my mind to pop up somewhere else. Miami and maybe Dallas are my next destinations, but when it came to it, my mind made up on *I'm going to Detroit*. Sara bought the ticket for me, and I caught a cab to the airport on my route; the plane I'm boarding is landing at Detroit. Ten thousand plus feet high in the sky, I was excited and looking forward to enjoy life in Montana.

CHAPTER 28

Fucking Detroit—I thought the fiends in California are some hardcore smokers, but these motherfuckers over here is off the hinge. All of 'em out the door, don't give a fuck about none but where the next hit is gonna come from, selling their mother's soul if they have a chance, just to get high, and I look nothing like their father. So if they don't give a fuck about their own parents who gave 'em life, so who am I for the crackhead to think differently of? It happened as soon as I was in the lobby. I was already being preyed on, and as they watch, the smokers knew I have no one to pick me up. I didn't have much, just my luggage, but that's not the point, I got jacked. The thing is, California smoker, don't go to the airport and stick out people as these motherfuckers do in Detroit. Yeah! The fiends get high and burn their own hair walking down the street, and the tweekers roam the night and chill out with trolls. But these dope fiends were high or needed to get high in Detroit. It's like they have superpowers and were not afraid of shit, and these motherfuckers were as fast as lightning strikes. All I did was get up, walk over to the phone booth to use the phone's yellow pages to look for a motel to book for a couple of days to check things out; but before I could even find a number to a hotel to call to make a reservation, I turn to look at my belongings, and they were not where I had left them. I turned again to double-check, and my luggage was long gone; with this incident, I had second thoughts about Detroit and decided against it and decided to go back to California. While I was waiting to board my flight to San Francisco, I came up with a better plan—New Jersey or Atlanta, but it was already too late, and I have to look into it later on. So I said, "Fuck it," and headed back to Modesto, the city of life that treated me hella bad, locked me up, and got me feeling sad; when you wanted time to go by fast, it is hella slow. This was the case for me with my waiting in the lobby with my only belonging gone; I still have my health and safety to worry about. So I can't even try to get some shut-eye because of the fear of the fiends because they mean smoking.

CHAPTER 29

Arriving at the San Francisco Airport, Sara was already there waiting, and since I didn't have any luggage, we headed straight to the parking garage. After paying the ticket, we were on the road heading for the Bay Bridge crossing, to go straight home. The date was April 4, about to turn the fifth. At midnight, which was my birthday, Sara broke the happiest and best birthday-present news ever. She began real shy and slow, "Honey, you want to know something?"

"Yeah, I do," I let out between a smile.

"I'm pregnant," she announced. I went lifeless on hearing my birthday news, and my soul returned from the grave by her kiss. Never before have I been excited like this. My heart was pumping fast and hard. I can't believe it. I'm going to be a father; I was full of joy. I leaned over and pulled her for a hug; having forgotten all about her carrying a child, and driving, we almost went off the 580.

I was so happy and full of bliss; I told her, "I love you, Sara, and gods, you and I, know I do." My spirit was awakened from the dead hope I've been waiting for since the death of Mona and my child. Finally it was coming true, and I smiled to myself, thinking of the future. I can't wait for my "one day" that I've been waiting for to arrive. All my bad feelings toward her were gone; I admired everything about her. She always was such an amazing girl with such a gift. She can listen to a song on the radio one time, and the next time she hears it, she can perfectly sing along. I was surprised as I recall the memory to when we were living on a Third Street apartment in Lowell, Massachusetts. The radio was playing. I was just lying with her in my arms, exhausted from the sex that I was so mad about, fucking her brains out; her head was resting on my chest, and she came twice that night—something that no one had ever done for her

---

before. Playing on the radio was "Killing Me Softly" by Lauryn Hill, and she sang a perfect song for me; but I don't think she knew it, because if she did, she probably wouldn't kill my unborn child. And along with the baby I'm also being buried alive, and I hated her for her evil deeds that I can't bring myself to forgive or forget. As soon as we got home that night, we had both forgotten about the baby inside, enjoying each other lustfully inside the car, creating the burn that can't wait till we get home, and it was on again. I love the way she flex her pussy muscle to suffocate my cock; it's like squeezing the life out of my dick. In the morning, Elisabeth awoke and found us on the floor where we passed out from the fuck. She came running, with sleep still in her eyes and all, tripping over pillow and blanket, to get on top of me, and at that moment I made up my mind to accept her as my own. Then it happened; as Sara talked to a couple of her friends who didn't give a shit about her, Sara in return took their advice and in turn did the unthinkable—lied to me about going out when what she really meant was, "I'm going to take the baby out." I was sad to the bones on hearing the lies, and I cried for my unborn child when the news came; and from this incident, my love for her has changed, because the way I see love is that love conquers all. How can someone say that they love you, when they are killing a part of you? And if this was how Sara wants to love me, by killing my baby and telling me lies about saying she's doing it for the best for both of us, I didn't need her love because my eyes see it differently. If you love someone, no matter the situation or predicament, you shouldn't give up on each other even when the future seems hopeless. I was stressed out about the abortion for a while, before I got over it, saying, "Fuck it, I don't need to be tied down with someone who's only half-ass loving me." so I let the pain come and accepted it and turned back to my old way, being my old self—only this time, if I get pulled over or stopped for anything, I'm heading to the county jail, no question, no answer. I was on the run.

CHAPTER 30

A lot of shit had happened within the few months that I went on the run. The scenery of the familiar surrounding seemed different. Even the hang-out spot has changed; all the homies mellowed out for some odd reason, and as for myself, I didn't give a fuck as I felt there's nothing for me to give a fuck about, or I have nothing or any reason to live. So I kept up with my gangbanging and other criminal activities; Sara, on the other hand, were having problems at home. The grandparents were fed up not with Sara but with my stupidity and took it out on Sara because she wouldn't stop seeing me, and for her disobedience, they kicked her out, forcing her to sleep in the car in the cold with me. Coming to the youth center, where I get my swell on working out to try and stay in shape, getting off the pull-up bar, I turned to see Sara; and eyes full of tears, she told me, "My grandparents are kicking me out." Seeing her crying got me to feel sorry for her. So I rented a house and had one of my Hit Squad buddies and his girl stay at the house; I told Sara, "I have a friend that we can go stay with for a while," so she wouldn't know everything about me. Sara, who had no other option, as her husband is gone, accepted my offer. From here on, our relationship was based on a game more than anything. I just can't bring myself to forgive her for rewarding me with a fuck, after she killed my unborn child. I didn't eat for days with all my taste buds gone out of my mouth. Losing all track of time, going around lifeless, I can't even get high no more. So I was bored and got involved in a heavier drug, digging myself deep into the world, and the dope game caught up with me; soon after, I got pulled over and was caught for a violation of parole. The board gave me a year max, and Sara was on the out, struggling by herself; and Elisabeth only made matters that much harder for her, but she managed to move to another house on her own. It was a studio, but it was a place she can call as her own while she worked as a YTT relay operator, and in between she came to visit me at the PSC (Public Safety

Center). Again, I found myself loving her all over, for the way she sacrificed her time to come and spend it with me in a little room with glass in between. One time as she was in a hurry, just got off work, and wanted to make it on time to see me, she didn't bother to pick up Elisabeth like she normally did. Alone with only the two of us, I asked her to play with herself for me, so she finger fucked herself for me to watch. I can still see how she banged herself. I finger, one, two, three, eyes low with each added finger. I got hard, and after the visit, I had to jack off to her from my memory of how she played with herself. I nut then I meditated, but no matter how hard I try to concentrate, my mind kept with the why question; I couldn't come to a clear conclusion as to what to do to stop thinking of her, wondering why I love Sara Long the way I do. I tried to reason with myself, as to why she was so very special, thinking hard, trying to find a way to bring myself to see the reason, but maybe it was because I was locked up, and Sara was the only female I saw. I would tell myself this, but my other self would tell me it couldn't be. I just didn't know what it was exactly. I guess it was 'cause of the way she had been constantly standing by my side, and that alone was enough to cover the sin of killing a part of me, because love covers all and is stronger than death. Heaven and hell can't separate love; to my understanding, love is above all else.

CHAPTER 31

Summer, winter, spring, and fall. I have to flip a whole calendar before it was my time to parole. I got released from the Donavan State Prison down in San Diego, catching the Hound once again, and I'm sick of it. Plus it reminded me to much of the gray goose that the CDC used for transportation. I hate the shit smell, the damn paper-thin jumpsuit, the shackle chain, the uncomfortable seat and ride. There ain't nothing fun when you're in trouble, but mistakes cost, and that's the price you have to pay. Coming home without any announcement, I had a plan to surprise Sara. Stepping out of the bus, I walked home from the bus station; besides, it was only about four blocks away. Once at the front door, I was about to knock on the door, but the little boy in me wanted to play the hide-and-seek game that we once used to play when we were young. Moving to the side window, to see if I can see anything, my eyes caught sight of Sara, so forever innocent and very lonely looking, sitting on the bed, reading *Diamond Boy*; on seeing her, I desired to have her in my arm, and I can't wait to hold her and instantly forgot about the game. I ran back to pound on the front door. When she looked through the peephole and saw my face, she must've went into shock, as it took her longer than usual for her to open the door. Still trying to catch her breath, one hand on her chest as the door swung open, I opened my arms for her to come to me and let us comfort each other. Our bodies touched, mouths locked, and moving backward, making our way to the bed, closing the door with my feet behind us without locking it, we hastily got undressed. By the time we were done getting our fuck on, Sara was running late to pick up Elisabeth from the day care, but being a good mother that she is, she didn't give a shit. Cum stain still fresh on her mouth and all, Sara didn't bother to even wash herself up, throwing the closest set of clothing she could find on, without underwear, throwing a few sprinkles of water on her hair. She was out the door to pick up her daughter. It was Friday, and I didn't have to report to my parole officer till Monday. So we spent the weekend fucking each other's brains out. And Monday, it was time to get back to my regular program. Sara went to work; I went to see my parole officer. But if it wasn't for her, I would have never checked in. She knew me and what I'm gonna do better than anyone else; she knew that if she didn't keep reminding me to make sure I go report, I wouldn't do it. She would always do her best to talk me into doing the right thing. Sometimes she even took me to see my party officer herself. She knew all my schedule, and she was on top of it, trying to help me get off parole. It worked for a while, but when she was closer to conceiving and her stomach was getting bigger, pregnant with Alexandria, my mind started to play a trick on me; and I began to make things hard for her, accusing her of being out fucking, calling to bother her at work, and watching her from a distance during her break time. She was having a hard time moving around. Sara, this time around, learned from her past mistakes and was determined to keep the baby; no matter what happened or what anyone had to say, she was gonna keep the baby, and true to her word, she did. When the baby was born, we agreed to name her Alexandria; and that Alexandria is you, my daughter, a blessing from God to soothe all of my agony from the unborn part of me that your mother killed.

Chapter 32

Meanwhile Sammie has become of age; she's ready to come and find her future husband to be (me) and claim me to herself as her heart had desired, so she persuades her mother to move out here to Modesto. As soon as she turns eighteen, true to herself and her word, she wasted no time in her quest of searching for me; her mother agreed to come along, but still there's a problem. Sammie only knows me by my real name, Tommy Ok, which didn't make things easy for her because down here in California, everybody has an a.k.a.; mine was Flea because of the way I was able to move around. Sammie arrived in Modesto with her mother who she threatened to leave behind if she's not gonna come along; and since Sammie is the only girl, and her mother's favorite, they both moved, leaving Map, who could have been my business partner—if it wasn't for the salt that could ruin/destroy the car if left sitting on it for long, and we couldn't find a buyer for it. So he went back to his nine to five, slaving his life away, making someone else money, while he's collecting pennies, hating himself for waking up every day, knowing that he has to be at work and without a choice as he has a family to support. Sammie on the other hand was searching high and low, from street to avenue, looking for Tommy Ok, and the people that know me by my real name are very few. She even moved into the heart of Khmer town, 620 Paradise. Sammie must've asked every resident that resided there, but no one was able to help her locate her Tommy Ok. A whole year passes by, and still no sign of Tommy Ok (me); and what makes matters worse, I was incarcerated at the time, serving a three-year sentence. But Sammie never lost hope and refused to give up, continuing to go on searching after what her heart has desired. She hang around, going against her own self, about giving herself a year's time. "This is the last year I'll hang around," she told herself the same lies the second time, and she has to cheat herself three times to have one of her dreams come true. So from her experience, I learned patience and endurance. There are other things that I admire her for, especially her love, and how she is willing to take the pain to make sure I get the pleasure. She was a good thang, a wonderful person to my life, and like all other good things, it didn't last. Because even God gives both blessing and adversity, testing the faith of all.

CHAPTER 33

Even though Sara is bearing my child, things between us aren't going too well. The communication was not there, and my drug-smoking habit picked up. I stay out late; and later, I don't work, barely fuck, never help out around the house, or watch the kid. Sara had it up to her neck, ready to get rid of the loser me; and during the heat of our argument, I manipulated her to tell me the truth about killing our baby, and I wanted her to answer, "Why don't you kill my baby that you are carrying too?"

She reassured me about keeping the child inside of her no matter what. "I'm keeping the baby." One thing lead to another. I heard what Sara was saying, but I pay no mind to none of what she said. I turned back to just being me, doing whatever the hell I want, how I want it, no matter the time and place, and everything else that was connected to me; I've been doing my own shit since I was a boy. If it wasn't bad enough, I sometimes would call pregnant Sara to come pick me up as I'm too stoned to even open my eyes sometimes or just too fucked up off of the combination of drugs to see straight. But I kept my using of drugs pretty low-key, and when I need to come down, I go to sleep. I smoke some weed and pop sleeping pills, and that'll do the job of knocking me out; after a while, this becomes a regular. Sara had it with my stupidity, and with her grandparents now offering her hospitality and a helping hand, she just said, "Fuck him"; she let it be known to me. Now the loc is on his own, and by myself, I went out of control, moving fast and strong with my habit. I got addicted to crack rock—cocaine, and followed by crystal. A colorless, odorless, tasteless, clear-as-blue-sky substance that if you try, you will see color, and the smell of shit will be on your body. It has the aroma of death and the bitterest taste of your life. I was hooked, lost and afraid to come home, but Sara would find me and continue to take care of me. When my tags expire on my car, she came and put it on for me, thinking that that's my only means of transportation; but I could easily place a phone call to Mr. Cooper and have my dead wife Kimberly's 911 on the next train to me anytime, but I didn't want to be rude, and I already know the reaping benefit of saying nothing, especially when you don't have nothing good or nice to say. It's best not to say anything. One day, as Sara was missing me too much, she came looking for me at the Dice, short for 620 Paradise. On seeing my beat-up white Buick; she knows that I was there, and she was right. I was in one of the apartments, shooting craps and hitting the GP (glass pipe), the weed bong, with music blasting; one of the little Hit Squad homies brought me the news of Sara looking for me. Looking out the window, I saw her coming with both hands holding her belly. She came, and when she got to the front door, she damn near kicked in the door. I ran to the back room, pretending like I was playing a game. Someone opened the door for her; I can hear her asking for me. She came to where I was; on seeing me, she said, "So this is a responsibilities of a father, ha?" I stayed quiet, and she got louder. My right mind told me to get up and walk away, but something came over me that day, maybe because of the madness or the embarrassment. It might be even the drugs and being deprived of sleep that irritated me. Yeah! I would have to say the drug! That's what everybody else would say, but I also blame myself, because I didn't prepare myself well enough for this to even happen. So it started with me, and I'm the one who fucked up, and I am able to admit that now when I couldn't back then. To me, that's a man, and every man is different including my self. That's why I live life my way, in the fast lane, because this is America.

CHAPTER 34

I was lying on the dirty, piss-stained mattress on the floor, holding a controller. Sara came and stood almost on top of me. I looked up and saw this. I throw the controller, pulling the game system with it; I got up to take hold of her and shock the shit out of her, demanding, "What the fuck do you think you're doing?" because a girl standing on top of a man is a form of disrespect in Cambodian culture. I must've shocked her a little too hard, that it sent pain to her belly to have her grabbing hold of it. With this, it was the straw that broke the camel's back, and once again, she walked out of my life. I should have ran after her and save what we have; but when you're hot, there's nothing you can do that is prudent, and from across the open area between the apartment complex, through the window, I watched Sara Long. She was crying her last cry, turning to see if I was coming after her; and when she saw me at the window, she yelled, "Come and get the rest of your fucking belongings out of my house, and stay the motherfucking away from me and my children." Hearing what she had let out made me felt different, along with the past action taken by her, leaving me when I needed her most. My mind automatically assumed that this bitch was trying to hurt me again, and this just added anger to my fury. I can't take it no more, and because of Sara, I was mad at the world, taking it out on everybody including my own self. Yes! Especially myself. With my mind made up to never go home to Sara Long or see her face ever again, I brought my mind to a "fuck it" solution. Don't get me wrong at times! I miss home, miss Sara, miss the children, and everything else that has any connection to her; since I didn't have no reason to keep on living in Modesto, I've decided to move to Tacoma, Washington, to be away from town, my peers, and the drug for a while. With a new mission and a new start in mind by myself, on the run and all, I stopped reporting in to see my parole officer. I didn't give a fuck no more; I felt I don't have nothing to live for, or anything to lose. At the time I had a Ford van '81 or '79 some shit, but that's a tough piece of machine with a 351 motor and double gas tanks. I started my long journey out on Freeway 99 and merge onto 5, then cruised all the way, nonstop, only one time to refill, and I didn't even cut off the engine. In Oregon, I was planning to start anew and do it on my own with no help from anyone, not even from Mr. Cooper. I was planning to advance my hands-on experience in building maintenance, sleeping in my van, taking a second job, and saving everything, eating food out of trash cans, buying nothing, using my saved-up capital to start my own business. Being my own boss was my mission. I wanted to accomplish something on my own. Besides, I learned that if you're not going to do it for yourself, no one else will. But all these were just my fantasies.

CHAPTER 35

Going northbound I-5, I have no place in particular in mind; I passed Redding and came to a small town called Weed, and anyone who smokes weed who saw anything that had to do with weed will get their attention turned to it. When I read the word, I said to myself, "Fuck it," and decided to pull over and smoke my head out, took a real-quick exit, and pulled over from the quiet road. I did; I was higher than the mountain that I was on. Lying back on the seat, I fell asleep; when I got up, I smoked another joint before I got back on the road, out of California and entering Oregon. Pass Crescent City, my gas needed to be refilled again, but I didn't because I had another half a tank to go and punched the old Econoline all the way to Eugene before I pulled over for gas; my mind turned to think about Chanrithy Him, the only other Cambodian author—of *When Broken Glass Floats*—that I know besides myself. Her story was all right. But it only touched me a little; matter of fact, I wasn't being moved. Maybe because I'm from where she's from and our view is the same, as we experienced and had been put through the same predicament and had a lot in common, that's why I'm not moved. Only on paper and with ink have we come to know each other and shared perspectives on how we see things for the better of our living conditions; in books, we expressed our opinions, but in real life, we never bumped heads. Shaking the thoughts of Chanarithy Him out of my head, I bring myself back to the gas station. Pulling into the Love gas station, I pulled up to the pump, not bothering to cut the engine and hop out to self-serve myself; but as I was taking off the gas cap, the gas boy, whom I know nothing about, yelled out from across the lot. "Hey! You can't do that." I was like what the fuck. I take it he was talking to someone else and reaching for the nozzle, but no, he was talking to me all right; and when he got done with the customer he was serving, and he came to me, he explained, "You can't pump your own gas here, that's my job."

"Job." Again, I was like what the fuck. But I told him, "Oh, I'm sorry. I didn't know you don't do self-service here because I'm from California."

"Oh, don't worry about it, I get it all the time. I mean if it's up to me, I rather have you pump your own gas, so my job will be easy," he responded politely, building rapport, trying to earn tips, which I did. He was a nice boy with wire-rim glasses, about two feet taller than my self, and almost ten years my junior I guess. He's probable trying to earn his college money so that he can make something of himself, but in the right way of going about doing it, and not like my way.

CHAPTER 36

Leaving Eugene and leaving Chanrithy Him, whom I've never met in person, behind, kind of got me to have a plan change. As I begin to ponder deep and long with the miles I'm traveling, I start to see my potential, my ability, and what I'm capable of doing. I know that for the individual that I am, I know I'm more than just a regular nine to five; and for my education, plus the experiences I have been through, I can see myself doing great things for myself and helping others who are less fortunate. And for the first time in my life, I was clear of my desire of becoming an entrepreneur with this discovery set in my mind. It gave me confidence in myself as I saw the possibility of a self-made millionaire. Yeah! I want to do it on my own. But what can I do, and who can help take me there? Those were my questions. Plus "it takes money to make money in America"; I had some capital investments but still lacked business skills, experience, and ability. To open and operate the business I'm interested in, I am still determined to give myself a try and make something out of myself, shaking the fact that I can't go legal out of my head, because I'm on the run from the law. I tried to work for cash for a couple of weeks, staying in my van by the school park on Thirty-eighth and Yakima, but the money flow was too slow; getting paid under the table washing dishes for the Chinese, the money was very little for my taste to like. I was forced to pull out my illegal shit. While inside my van, smoking my weed before going to my second job of toilet cleaning, looking out the window, I observed a white man walking the park, smoking a joint; I knew because of the smell and the way he smoked it, so I waited till he came around to where I parked, before I opened the passenger door in an unthreading way, backed myself up, and invited him in for some green. "Excuse me, you care to join?" I offer, showing him the pint. "It's all right! I'm just someone who happen to enjoy smoking weed," I reassured him, hitting the light blunt, choking. I passed it to him, who looked around before taking the offered blunt and stepping inside the van. His name was Steve, an ex-marine. So we got the smoking, coughing, talking, and getting acquainted. We came to have similar problems and similar interests between us, so we're related. I got comfortable and told him of my plan, and I loved nothing more than to grow bud by the tons, I told Steve; but he convinced me that my plan is a weak one, because he got a cousin who lives on the other side of the border in British Columbia, Canada, who grows weed. The idea of someone growing it for me sounds too good to be true, but I was desperate, and with the desire to be a millionaire as soon as I can, I joined hands with Steve and his plan; together we went to talk to different people, potential buyers that Steve actually used to deal with and tried to bust but couldn't get close to anyway! The cousin who I didn't bother to give a shit about was supposed to be tending the crops and almost ready with the first harvest. My investment got less to nothing in return; my sweat-earning money is running real low, and fast on top of that, Steve told me that we had to relocate up closer to Canada, to Bellingham. So we can be next to the border to make things easy for everyone. So one thing lead to another, and it turned out that I ran into my own trap; Steve turned out to be a law-enforcement officer, a U.S. Marshal who was on duty, doing undercover work in a sting operation. I got busted; I thought he was joking when he told me that I was under arrest, until I was sitting in jail in the middle of nowhere. That I believed what was happening was real, I thought of all my options, but I can't seem to find a way out of this mess; without no one to turn to, the loc is on his own. From the Washington jail, I tried to call Modesto, collect to Sara; and she, too, said, "No!"

"You have a collect call from Tommy," and the phone went silent. Fuck it. I have only one choice left, and I took advantage of it.

As I remember Mr. Cooper's phone number by heart, I placed a collect call to him, and his secretary Linda accepted my call, asking, "What happened? Why you have to collect call?" By now, she hasn't learned that the only time I call is when I'm in trouble. I got some relief, as well as the sad news. As Mr. Cooper announced the fact of Father Robert passing away, going to the abyss of what he believed to be God's Kingdom, I was mad at myself as I can't be there for him on his last day, to pay him respect before he rested in the ground to never return. I have to prolong my court date, waiting for Mr. Cooper to fly up from Lawton and bail me out of all this. Because I was facing an international charge, things looked ugly for me; the U.S. attorney offered me a twelve-year deal.

CHAPTER 37

I was lying on my metal rack after busting out some couple of hundreds of push-ups, exhausted, reading, maybe rereading, the Commander Rommel, as I was interested on knowing how the war was waged out and what strategies were being put into use; also, I'm trying to bring my mind to the next level of thinking, seeing, viewing, and doing things. The thumb-size grill-bars door slid open, and my name was being called for the first time. "Tommy Ok" was being called for something else beside court; on hearing my name, I jumped down from my bed and ran to stick my head out. The officer told me, "Get dressed and come out, lawyer visit." I was excited that I had a visitor; I already knew who it was, because that was the only visit that I knew was gonna come—from Mr. Cooper, who was here to see and help me out. I saw him sitting in the little box room with glass in between the room, waiting for me, Mr. Cooper. He, too, seemed to turn old overnight from the death of Father Robert. They were more like family than just business associates, friends from the service. He was crying as he delivered the news. I wanted so much to reach over and comfort him with his sadness, but all I got to do for him is feel his pain. Once all the sad shit was out the window, the first thing that came out of my mouth was, "I need a lawyer, and I don't want nobody else beside you to represent my case."

"But, Tommy, I'm a civil lawyer, and not a criminal."

"I know, but I only trust you with my freedom and my life, especially now, that my father's gone." Mr. Copper appeared disappointed as he took a deep sighing, feeling sorry for himself for taking Father Robert's offer to look out for me and care for me. But whatever it was, he sadly agreed to help me. And the result from his help, he got me six months federal time and got me transferred to Oklahoma Federal Prison. And I got released three months after I arrived there; I moved back to stay in Lawton for about a year with Sue Upchurch. The townhome I once lived in was now sold. I was living with Sister/Professor Sue Upchurch; she got me taking Bible courses, but religion was dead to me since Father Robert's death. Me and Sue, we fucked and fucked a lot. She's a horny freak. It's like fuck, fuck, fuck was the only thing on her mind—in the morning, after school, after she's done her teaching; she probably got her professorship. There was just something about her that turned me off. The feelings were not there, and the only need I had was to get away from her; I can no longer stand her and can't wait to be discharged from parole. But when it came to it, as I was fed up with Upchurch, I said, "Fuck parole." I had a soldier mentality, and with that, I was out of Lawton, heading back to Modesto. Only this time, I did my own driving, the 911 Porsche that my wife left behind for me. Only to have what's left of my Kimberly towed away a couple of days later as I got into a high-speed chase. Losing the 911, I also lost the last piece of my wife who got me here to America, the land of the free, with plenty of opportunities to turn any dream into reality, expect for mine; at least that's how I felt at the time.

CHAPTER 38

On my journey, my mind was full of Sara and the newborn; for some strange reason, I can't wait to see them, but I only got disappointed. When I got to Modesto, I didn't believe my friend about my Sara Long when he told me what she's been up to. "Yo! Flea! I saw your baby momma with a black guy, homie! What's up with that?" The homeboy Tone wanted to know.

"You sure that's my baby momma?" I wanted to make sure, because part of me still loved her. I wanted to also kinda show off my macho to the little homie and said, "You're mistaking her."

"Come on, homie, why would I want to tell you some bullshit for?" he said, to remove my doubt; I still didn't believe him but didn't say nothing else. I have a plan to surprise her with my '79 911 collectable Porsche; *punk bitch,* I called her in my head, and again I couldn't wait to see her and her black man together. Fuck it; she's not more important than my weed, I told myself after I reasoned with myself. Heading to Turlock to the connection house, I grabbed me an ounce of some killer weed from my Mexican people; since at the time I didn't have a license and was on the run, I got my crimie to do the driving and would lie about my name if we got pulled over for any reason after we scored our weed. While I tried to roll us up a fat blunt, it happened that Lice was turning too sharp as he got nervous when he saw the cops sitting inside the patrol car; he wanted to pull over and stop when the pigs mashed up on us, but I told him, "This is a Porsche, fool, we got weed and I'm on the run, and you're talking about pulling over?"

"What, are you, crazy?"

I yelled at him, "Hit it, fool!" And he let the pedal hit the metal. The mobster mashed out, doing 65 on the city's 25 and 35 streets; the speed hit up to 165 on the freeway. Looking back, there were more and more cops' cars on our trail. I told Lice, "I can't afford to get caught." As I thought about the 911, I felt the loss of both the car and my freedom. Thinking fast, I quickly came up with a fuck-it solution; again I gotta run. Coming fast on northbound 99, approaching Modesto, there were cops waiting for us at every exit. Think quick; there was a diesel in the middle of the right lane, and I saw an opportunity and told Lice, "If you can cut real sharp in front of the diesel, and make it up the ramp, we will lose a lot of the cops, and we might have a chance to get away." He saw what I saw. He hit the hand brake hard, spinning the 911 around and swerving and swaying awkwardly in front of the eighteen-wheeler who was pulling the horn, and behind the waiting CHP that went past the exit. We went up the ramp, coming fast; it must have been at least 80 when we turned left on I, going over the path, running another red light, making right on Third. We were heading for Oak Street. Lice can't slow down fast enough to take the left turn. The Porsche's tires were screaming, and we ran into a parked car, almost knocking me out, but I was conscious enough to manage to open the door; the car bounced off the parked car and hit a parked boat on the other side of the street and smashed into an old tree, smashing not only my Porsche but also my leg. The car had smoke coming out the hood. I was saying to myself, "Shit! I gotta get out of here," but my door was stuck because of my big-ass Raiders jacket. So Lice had to pull me out through the driver-side door.

"Come on, fool," he urged me. The siren was getting closer, and we had to get far, as far as we can from the crime scene. Helping one another, heading for the garage-door fence, it was too high, and I couldn't make it over, but that was no problem when you got a partner like Lice. Hanging at the top of the fence, on his belly, Lice reached down for me. I gave him my hands, and with a little help from me, he was able to pull me over. I fell hard on the ground, knocked the wind out of my lungs, and I couldn't even move. Leaning against the wood fence, I told Lice to run, but he said, "No! You're my crimie, and I'm not going to leave you."

"Are you stupid or what?" I barked with heavy breathing.

"Yeah, stupid enough to get caught or get away with you," he reassured me. But I couldn't move, and he said, "We're going together," and we were only twenty-five feet away from where the car crashed. Luckily, there was no dog inside, as we used the doghouse as our hideout. We could hear dispatch on the cops' radios, and when that died out, came the beeping sound of the tow truck to tow my pride and joy away, taking the only tie of Kimberly away from me; I cried.

CHAPTER 39

The next day, with both of us still nursing our injuries, we made it to Mellis Park on Martin Luther King, California, to spy on Sara Long; and sure enough, to my surprise, I saw my bitch with Elisabeth and Alexandria in the stroller, walking hand in hand with her new man. They seemed happy together. So I decided it was best to go on with my life, but I didn't get far, and only deeper into my dope world, smoking my life away; and like water in the desert, my money dried up, leaving me to be in desperation, calling me to do desperate things, and nothing turns out for me and only got me going down to the lowest point of my life. Let me tell you, from where I came from, to the blessings I had back in Lawton with good people, but I chose to run away from the goodness and lost it all. I tried to force things to work out; it was a time of confession and a moment of self-searching, but things were hard for me. I couldn't seem to find the answer. I tried to do the right thing, going to the fields and picking peppers and other products with the border brothers in the field under the hot, brewing sun and quickly learned it was not for me; so I switched to work with plastic cups in a factory then switched to metal and then glasses, but this, too, didn't work out for me. And I tried the paper and the press, but nothing worked. The only good thing was that I had received a lot of knowledge and skills from those jobs, but at the same time, I was on my own, and working for pennies in construction was no fun. On top of the list of my opportunities of making money, there was none that I had the avenue to turn and find support for myself, except for one, and that one was to grow weed—lots and lots of weed at various spots, and from my last experience, I told myself not out of American soil; this time I have to do everything alone, with no car, no cash—more of a dead person than alive. Down to 119 lbs., riding my bike around to collect junks and trade them for dope, I was what you call a dummy; I was down to the very bottom, having nothing to care for. I slept with bums under the bridge, and by small rivers, later on at any place that was suitable to pass out. It could be in a box, by the dumpster, park bench, abandoned house, you name it. I gave up on living and only went through the motions, with no kind of feelings whatsoever about anything, not even eating, and only had whatever lunch that I ate at the Salvation Army that were being served from 11:45-1:15 for the homeless. I once passed out by their building after they fed me, and one of the volunteers brought me a blanket, whom I thought was an angel.

CHAPTER 40

It was the 1990s, during Khmer New Year, during the month of April and also my birth date that Sammie finally got a break, as she ran into one of my close friends that I knew when I first moved out here to Modesto, who I kept in touch with, or you can say someone nice that I used and abused because I only go to their house when I needed to get cleaned up. One day, after I showered and ate, I couldn't watch TV as I felt the need to get high and was irritated. I took off, leaving all my belongings behind and not knowing who the dirty backpack belonged to. My good friend Reo unzipped my bag and went through the paperwork and read my information and found out that my real name is Tommy Ok, and Sammie asked this girl whose house I go to, to shower, as Sammie saw the new face inside of Engle Market. "Excuse me, but do you live here in Modesto for a long time?"

"I guess, since 1985," Reo replied.

"I don't know how to put this, but I'm looking for someone by the name Tommy Ok." Reo's facial expression changed on hearing my name; Sammie again must've known and pressed on, "You see, I'm from Lowell, Massachusetts. And I've moved down here, looking for my future husband. So if you know where Tommy's at, please help me," and Reo helped her; the two of 'em got to talking, and Reo set up everything for us, arranging a place for us to meet, and she picked the temple on Paradise Rd. when we came face-to-face. She was nothing compared to the Sammie of old. She has grown more gorgeous, was tall, not fat, but stupidly thick. I kinda remembered her, but she remembered me well, even though I have aged, and my weight changed. There was something that she remembered of me for her to be so sure that it was me with no question, no answer. Sammie took this little lost puppy (me) home, and she washed me up, fed me, cared for me, and gave me money to buy dope, pussy to fuck, and got herself pregnant along the way. When she was too big to go to work, we moved in with her mother, who disliked me down to my shit. Everything about me disgusted Ruth, but I just didn't know how to give a fuck anyway! Nine months later, Cryxtal came out at DMC, with me passed out on the chair in the delivery room, leaving Sammie to cry her pain alone in her labor, and a couple of months later, she bore a child again. It was the saddest time for us, a real bad time to get kicked out, as Sammie chose me over her own mother. Because to her, it was love above everything else in her life, to go even against her own mother with her belief, and to be real with her love, she suffered along with me.

CHAPTER 41

The sky outside looked like it was threatening to rain; blue was replaced with gray, with no late-morning sunshine. Taking nothing but the clothes on our back and Cryxtal's bottle, Sammie started the MVP. The minivan had been good to us, and so was the weather, but as we didn't learn our lesson from the ants, we didn't prepare ourselves for the winter. Losing our van to smoking dope and playing the 4-5-6 dice game, Sammie put the pink slip into the pond and didn't have money to get it out on time, and with all of her credit cards all maxed out, and the life of a dope fiend is no fun and game for no one, not the dealer nor smoker; both are serious about something—for the dealer, the money, and for the smoker, the high. And from what I have witnessed, I vowed to never bring myself down to the smoker's point; not did I break my vow with myself. I involved another life into my smoking activities. Now instead of one habit, I have to support two, on top of Cryxtal's milk, diaper, and clothing. We would go beg for her milk, using her as bait. We came to our senses a couple of times, and my Sammie would go back to work; but that, too, didn't last long as her habit kicked in harder than mine, and we were back to square one, smoking our life away and down to pushing Cryxtal in the shopping cart with a throwaway pillow that we picked up along the road as we walked around, and we had a thin blanket for her just a little bigger than a bath towel. The cart was her home, her bed, and her playground was inside the cage, while Sammie and I got high in the alleyway as we went around picking cans. Cryxtal was a very understanding baby, and she seemed to see with adult eyes and knew everything. Communicating with her was easy; when we talked to her, she understood. As she has a cold nose and eyes running with no milk, coughing her little lungs out and not old enough to eat, we would feed her stale bread. Other babies would gag and throw up, but not my Cryxtal. One thing about her, she always loves the park; and since we didn't have nothing for or to give her, the least we can do was be at the place where she loves, and it worked out as we used the park bathroom to smoke our dope. But sometimes the park was too cold or wet, or we're at a friend's house too far away from the park that we can't take her to it; living with other people, I learned real quick that shit didn't last, and we never failed to be kicked out. Sooner or later those you live with will be fed up with your shit and will tell you to hit the road. So from Manteca, on Airport Way, we walked all the way to West Lane onto Hammer Lane, with our pipes hiding inside the inner pocket, and a small bag of dope tucked in between my ass cheeks because I was afraid that we might lose the last of our shit, or the cop might find it if we're stopped for whatever reason.

CHAPTER 42

"Hey! Homie, I think it's time for you to get up and go find someone else to live off of. My parents need to use the garage for the new car that they'll be picking up later on," my so-called friend said, after I told him that the twenty sacks of dope was gone, not even finished with the last round of our smoking session. I went to bed and as quickly was woke up by my good friend Joe, not even fully awake out of sleep; I got dressed into my unwashed clothes for a couple of weeks already. Sammie, whose eyes were full of shit that was seeping out between the lids, she didn't bother to wipe it away, getting Cryxtal's things together. Her stomach was beginning to show, but she had no problem moving, and when I tried to complain to her about walking, she told me, "It's okay! Walking is supposed to help your labor." There's no doubt in my mind that this girl didn't love me, and I loved her too very much for bringing herself down real low for the love she had for me, to be at my level of being a dope fiend and all. Slowly going, we must have walked two million; almost the whole day, we moved with little rest. When we got to Hammer Lane, it was already getting dark, and we still didn't know what to do or had any place to go in particular. So again we used Cryxtal as bait to get enough money to catch the bus back to Modesto or get us a room for the night. We needed something like $17 for the fare, and within the hours that we panhandled while we split up, with Sammie and Cryxtal at Wendy's, and me washing windows across the street at a gas station, we had enough for the fare, food, and some left for our drug, not thinking about the baby's milk. I came up with $52, but Sammie and Cryxtal did better, $97 in one hour. This profession has become our way of life, along with my old trade pulling cans and bottles out of the trash; collecting cans and bottles was money. Sometimes we would find so much, that Cryxtal had to sleep on top of the cans and bottles, while Sammie and I took turns hitting the glass pipe. Sometimes we would leave her in an abandoned house with her bottle filled for her, and she would wake up by herself, and instead of crying when she was awake and didn't see us, she played by herself, waiting for us to return, like she knew we would; this was the saddest time for us, with only worries and misery on our minds. The predicament forced us to once again come to our senses and cut down on our smoking a little, and we were able to get ourselves into a studio on Washington St., and the studio turned into a smoking chamber for everyone—all hours, day or night, nonstop. A couple of hours of sleep is all I get sometimes; in a month's time period, I get to shut my eyes one hour. No more begging or picking cans and bottles. That trick was over. I moved up to serve a little some-some, and that some-some got us by and at the same time got us evicted back to the street with Sammie about to be due anytime, but the smoking didn't stop.

CHAPTER 43

Sammie and I were talking, and we came to an agreement that we should stay as close to DMC (Doctors Medical Center) as possible to make things more convenient; for when she's ready to go into labor, we're there. The only trouble was that the dope man was too far; he's all the way across town on the west side, and what did we do? Like a dummy, we caught the MAX (Modesto Area Xpress) to downtown and got on another bus on our way to the connection house. On the bus we got everybody covering up their noses because we smelled bad, worse than a dog, but we didn't give a shit. My shirt has black burn holes in 'em and black spots all over, especially on the front side, from me using it to wipe the pipe clean of the black smokes so I can see the drug inside the glass bubble. I used my shirt to wipe off the GP (glass pipe) all the time. My head smelled like straight shit, and so was Sammie; she scratches her head more than ever. Maybe she had lice; and my feet had holes, and in between the crack and sole are open sores, a result from never letting my feet breathe any fresh air. How can I, when everywhere I go, I'm afraid to take off my shoes, for the fact of the death aroma. I, myself, knew it was superstinking, and I had the same pair of shoes like forever. In wintertime my feet get wet and freeze; Sammie had to wrap trash bag around her feet, and we managed to keep Cryxtal dry using the plastic from the furnisher dumpster around the chest, and we get clothes from anywhere that we can find it, especially if without paying for it. On occasions, we would go to the blood bank and sell our blood by the pint for fifteen dollars so that we can score our drugs. We didn't believe in spending money on nothing else but the drugs. Getting off at one of the stops on Paradise Rd., we walked; and we were about two blocks away from the connect house, when Sammie started to feel the pain, and just our luck, the bus had rolled out. Looking around, I found no one and only Cryxtal next to Sammie. I ran across the street to the little market

---

next to the burned-down Pizza Hut and used one of the pay phones that were lined up along the wall. 911, the dispatcher answered my call. "Yes!"

"I have a lady who's ready to go into labor, and need an ambulance." I gave her the address, "Paradise and Vermont." Stupid me, instead of staying with Sammie and taking care of Cryxtal, I told her, who was in great pain, to "watch Cryxtal and hold on while I ran to the connection house down the street to grab some shit!"

Sammie said, "No!" But I went anyway, and when I got back, Sammie and Cryxtal were gone, and to only one place—that is, the DMC. Calling for a cab, my destination was Pep Boys on McHenry; I planned on ride and run 'cause I have no money to pay for the fare. That was what I did.

"Hey! I'm gonna call the cop!" the cab driver yelled after me, when he knew my intention.

CHAPTER 44

After checking at the security front desk of the birth center, I registered as Sammie's neighbor and not as the baby's father. The fat guard picked up the phone and buzzed the double door open to let me in to see Sammie. I got in the delivery room in time to see my Cryxtal sitting there on the cherry-colored leather chair by herself, so innocent and harmless. And the head of my Diamond was about to come out. I was scared shitless, as I had both the GP and the dope in my possession, but luckily they didn't check. I looked at Cryxtal and turned to Sammie, who was in much pain, and on seeing me, she managed to smile, because she was happy that I made it, and in time to witness Diamond enter the world. I recalled her telling me, "I've been away from you long enough, and now that I found you, I'm going to stay close to you as possible, and if drug is what you want to destroy and kill yourself with, then out of love I'll do it with you, only you, and just you I live for, and I'll die with you, because my love for you is stronger than death." It was stupid of me to take advantage of her and never show her no kind of appreciation. Instead of trying to find a place for my newborn and my newly delivered mother Sammie to recover, I used my time to smoke crystal; matter of fact, we started together in the hospital bathroom. I told Sammie to try to stay in the hospital as long as possible, but the longest that she was allowed to stay was three days; and within that three days, I would clean out the cart of the baby's milk, diaper, towel, clothing, cloth, and everything else that I was able to sneak out past the security guard from the supply cart. I was scared at first for stealing from the hospital; but after the first day and first load, I got used to it, and by the time she was released, we had three months worth of milk for our deprived infant. Even with this head start, we still fell behind to the point where we almost have to put Diamond up for adoption. But Sammie showed me that we were better human beings than that. Coming to an agreement, even though she didn't fully agree about us leaving town, but the fact that I'll be away from drug alone, Sammie was with it, and willing to give it a try. Whether it was going to work out as planned or not, which it never did anyhow—she knew it; but still, never once did she gave up on love, the love of her life that she was gonna treasure to the end.

CHAPTER 45

It didn't take long for the agreement to be broken; quitting my plastic assembly line as the pay was not worth it and to go back to the panhandling lifestyle because we were able to make more that way, we both had a child to use as bait to reel suckers in giving us their hard-earned money. And like old habits are hard to break, I still go back to my begging ways from time to time, especially when I found myself missing Sammie. Maybe that was what had been a part of my life that had made me the individual that I am today, and I miss it because I miss my true love Sammie. Within a month, we managed to get ourselves a bucket, run-down Toyota Corolla '82 and moved back to Modesto from Dublin. We had about $750 for our trap, also a lot of dope. I'm surprised I didn't overdose yet, with as much dope as I've smoked. We were moving out of state going to Oregon; I had a plan to grow bud by the ton. I remembered the mountain from the previous trip that I took and had checked out before. Like the apple-seed guy, Jonny, whatever the fuck his name was, I had a sack of weed seeds that I was going to throw everywhere up in the Oregon mountains. So far, we didn't get far, and the piece-of-shit bucket was overheating. "Motherfucker," I said, "this is great, on the run, and two babies, this picture don't look too good." I could have easily taken a car with a screwdriver, but having all the drugs and a gun for the purpose of protecting the crops, it was not a good idea to be caught in a stolen ride; that only meant jail. So I went and stashed everything away by the bush along the freeway, and we took off, walking. We didn't get far when the highway patrol pulled up behind us and turned on his light, hitting his siren, getting us to turn and look. Right away he knew that was our car back there broken down. He was a real nice officer who was thoroughly professional. His name is Richard Corona Wonderful. Yes! Wonderful, under fine authority representative, protecting and serving the community.

"You guys can't be walking, it's dangerous," the officer warned us, as he stepped out of his patrol car. I was for sure I was in trouble, but Mr. Wonderful respects the right of every citizen's privacy that he didn't bother to try and run a check on our names, with only one mission in his mind, "to protect and serve the community." I have much praise for him. Mr. Richard Wonderful and his partner helped me out, when everybody else was just flying by, and occasionally, someone would honk at us without stopping. Opening the back door of the patrol vehicle, he told us to be careful getting in.

Once we got going, he asked if we needed help with anything beside gas. I kept quiet and let Sammie do all the talking; and when he tried to talk to me, Sammie advocated for me, saying, "He don't speak too good of English." The officer laughed and joked around with Sammie in a way that if he was given a chance, he would fall in love; his easygoing and encouraging way really lifted her spirits up as he was telling her how strong she was to be able to take care of three babies, and one of them was a big one.

"I admire that about a woman," he conceded. I must've passed out, because I didn't remember hearing anything else of their conversation and was awakened by Sammie in front of Shari's.

Chapter 46

I opened my eyes to see the entrance of Shari's Restaurant; and Officer Richard Wonderful put his cruiser on port, went to the trunk of the patrol car after letting us out, and he gave each Diamond and Cryxtal a teddy bear, lifting everybody's spirit up including mine. And I believe that because we have an officer like him out there patrolling the streets, that's what makes America the greatest society on earth; as if this wasn't enough, he bought us cold drinks to cool our throats. He thought that we didn't have any money. He went in to Shari's personally and out of his pocket ordered us something to eat, telling the employee there by the name of Desiree the situation, and requested for her to help us out as much as possible. While Sammie and the kids were eating, I went across the street over to the 76 gas station; first and foremost, before I did anything, I went inside the store to ask for permission to panhandle. The four-eyed clerk was nice enough to let me do whatever I needed to do, just as long as I didn't bother nobody or start any trouble with anyone. I gave him my word, "You will not have any problem, sir." I thanked the nerd and went out. The first man I approached, a white man in a big new white GM truck, I stated, "Excuse me, sir, my car is overheating on the freeway, and I'm trying to get enough money to fix it, so I can get to where I'm going. I'll even get your windows for you if that would get you to help out." The man pondered and self-talked with himself; a short second later, he started to talk to himself, "No! No! No!" He kept on repeating too, and when I finally asked him, "Well, sir, can you help me out?"

"No! I don't believe you have a car breakdown anywhere, or you from anywhere else, you live around here so I'm not gonna be fooled." I was like, what the fuck, and I thanked the man and moved on to another.

"Excuse me, sir, do you happen to have a gas can?" The reason why I wanted a gas can was so I can better persuade people because people go by what their eyes see. Another white guy with his partner went into the store. I approached him when he came back out. "Do you have a gas can I can have?" And he looked at me up and down. I offered to get the windows. "All I needed is a gas can, my car ran out of gas," I lied. The guy with the neon green hat went to the back of the van and pulled out a one-gallon plastic can out for me, and it happened that his partner that was with him with the same color hat came out of the store; when his partner told him my story, he was sold, and the gas can was mine with good-luck wishes from both of 'em. Now I have something to work with. The third man I approached, his name was Mr. Don Woods. I don't know what came over me to tell Don the truth about my situation, but I did; and the result was, at first he gave me $7 and asked me, "Is that enough?"

"If you want the truth, no, but it'll help!" I replied.

"So how much do you really need?" Don asked.

"What I need is to get my bucket radiator fixed, and not so much of the gas," I told him.

"So why are you holding a gas can then?"

Again I told him the truth, "That's because, just like what is happening with you right now, you give me money for gas, because you see evidence in my hand that I needed gas versus if I have nothing." I went on, "I didn't mean anything or harm anyone, and just trying to get enough money to have my car fixed."

To my amazement, Mr. Don nodded his head in agreement, pondering, before he said, "You know what, I like your style, and your way of doing things. So why don't we do this?" He offered with a question, "Where's your car at?" I told him northbound; he told me no problem, and he asked me again, "So do you need gas or your radiator fixed?" as he wanted to be sure. I explained the situation of how I don't know anyone in the surrounding areas and all. Mr. Wood knew that my need of help was genuine; he told me to get in the van with him, and we went to pick up my family from Shari's. She had just finished eating, and Sammie tried to stuff Cryxtal, because it could be a long while before the next meal came around.

CHAPTER 47

Mr. Woods was ahead of us. He had already called a tow truck and had the Corolla delivered to his house so that his mechanic friend could fix the car for us. His house was a beauty—a dream house, three-car garage, two stories, stony colored, with the stone fence to harmonize the view of the oak double door. Don introduced us to his wife; she turned from feeding her children and waved. Don fixed my car with his business credit card and sent us out on our journey with $100—half $50 cash and half $50 check made out to Sammie—along with a phone number and the assurance that we can come back to visit anytime. But like all good things, it never lasted, and leaving the Woods family behind without a chance of once returning for a visit, we ran into another set of troubles. I've been waiting impatiently to smoke some shit, and it was hiding back where the car was overheating. Going back to look for it, that was the first thing we did, when we left the Woods's house. We backtracked; I found my stash and once again headed out. The need for the drug was so urgent that my body was shaking that I almost couldn't drive; I can't wait to hit the pipe. As Sammie loaded it up, she melted it down for me, and once it cooled down, she took hold of the steering wheel so I can hit the pipe. One hit, two hits, three hits, that shit makes my hairs stand up and makes me want to take a shit, and when the crystal attacks you, you can't wait to get to the no-rest area. So we pulled over and slowly exited a deserted-looking road, and together we smoked under a lonely tree; once our eyes beamed up, we headed out again. We went without stop, only for gas. Passing Redding, and into Mountain Shasta, we paid a visit to the national park and got lost for days, going up and down the hills, with clouds of dust trailing behind. The going seemed like round and round; we came to the volcano that was still smoking, with little dead twigs growing out of it, all black like the ground. We stopped and got a good look; yes, it was round and round we go because it was the second time we had been at the volcano.

Going again, we came to a guard post; thank God the ranger helped us out, guiding us as to which way to go to get off the mountain. It was like the ghost of Sokhan Pring was haunting us and wanted us to be there with him, refusing us from leaving, but what a relief as we recognized the road that we entered from. Going again northbound, we pulled off in Reka and curved around right to come to this little stream, from which you can see salmons running up the streams, and there were tons of them. We brought Cryxtal out to watch the fishes, and she was enjoying her view; and while she was doing that, us parents took turns hitting the glass pipe and got into an argument about the shit, as I worried that the supplies might run dry. But upon realizing that I was getting away from Modesto to also get away from the drug, I apologized to Sammie; and we made up by rocking the toys, putting baby Diamond to sleep so that our nuts wouldn't be disturb. It was a good nut, I must admit.

CHAPTER 48

So far, I haven't made nothing out of myself because of the drug, and the lack of education didn't help. I began to hate my own self for treating myself badly. I needed to do something quick, fast, and in a hurry, but nothing came to mind as my tweeking mind pondered days on end. The crystal numbs all my brain cells, making it impossible for my thoughts to connect to any result. I looked like hell, and I had two young pups to look after. So I forced myself and brought myself to think, maybe God put a mark on me like he did with Abel, and that is to be a vagabond flea with no place in particular to call as home, going from one place to the next, because so far since birth, I've been around the globe, and still I have no place to call as home. Nothing changed in America from when I was in Cambodia. I can understand how you can get lost in America; but Cambodia, the country only the size of Oklahoma State, can make me lost for decades. Thinking back, maybe it was because I was young. But I hated those rebels. Coming back to myself, I started to see America from different eyes. In the jungle there was no hope, and the only chance I had was to survive. But in the United States, there's always a future; I saw opportunity, and lots of it, and that whatever it is you want to do or be, it's up to you. And I wanted to make something out of myself. So I tried to come up with a possibility, but to no satisfying outcome. Forcing myself to come up with something, I decided I'm sticking to my plan—and that was to go to Cotton Grove, Oregon, to grow my crops. We were excited; Cotton Grove made my heart beat out of rhythm, and studying the mountain brought me flashbacks of the jungle I was once lost in. I had to force myself to believe, "I've been here before, and five months from now I'll be filthy rich and away from the woods." For the mean time, we went out begging, but not to the point where we'll be recognized because we were supposed to be invisible. We rented a motel right across from the shopping plaza that has the Sav-Way supermarket and the U.S. Bank. That night I went to bed early 'cause I knew I had a long hard trip ahead of me tomorrow. It was a two-bedroom motel. We left the babies in one room and rocked the other, before I cummed in her mouth and passed out. I loved the way she sucked on my cock; she was a real sperm clearer. Sammie's own words were "sperm sponge." I asked her, "How?"

"Because if I'm not sucking you with my pussy, I do it with my mouth, and my asshole too," she said. I smiled 'cause it was funny to me. She smiled back and finished with, "That's true," and rolled over like a good puppy to take it in her ass and cleaned me up afterward because of its smell.

CHAPTER 49

I was up early at 4:00 AM dawn with Sammie already on the cock. Pushing her away, I hopped in the shower, and I was ready. Going over my supplies, Sammie packed Diamond and Cryxtal into the car to go drop me off and to drive the car back to Cotton Grove once I was dropped off at the spot; the little 1.8 machine is having trouble going up the hill and almost couldn't make it to the top where I wanted to start working, dropping the seeds. Luckily the bucket did make it to the top, and we kissed. I watched her drive away, before I began to work my way down. Sammie kept asking, "Are you sure you're gonna be all right?" If only she knew what I've been through, she'll understand I was one of the dead three hundred Spartans came alive; I'll be all right with anything, and this here was a piece of cake. Oh, if only that was true, because the work was backbreaking, and it took me a whole day in the mountain planting the seeds. Luckily the ground was softened a little by the water that poured down from the sky all season long, and that was the main reason I chose that particular area, because of the self-watering, to make my job that much easier. I let five weeks go by and came back to pinch the first internode and added nitrogen, protein, and calcium; I didn't return until twelve weeks later, to prune and fertilize. Just when my plant was blooming real nice, at the same time, it also gave out odor. Soon even the rain didn't help; the smell went out of control and could be detected by any noses from miles away. That meant danger from authority, and I wasn't going to stick around to find out that I have a chance to get a trunk full of the premature weed; and I managed to make enough to get by with my smoking for a while, but as fast as the money came, it was faster for the money to go. The dollar was easy, and we made enough to purchase for ourselves a Pathfinder SUV (Nissan). The rest was up in smoke. Soon we became broke again, and it was time for me to pull out some other plan. I did and almost blew up myself along with the wrong mix of chemicals that I threw in together—the chemical, which I believed to be the meth ingredient, as I was trying to make some crank. Half of my body was burned, as well as my face, and my hair got caught on fire. This took place in Little Delhi. Luckily there was a canal running behind the house, where I was going to dump everything into once I was done, but it didn't turn out as planned. I was lucky I made it out of there alive by going down to the canal. I don't know how far I got before I came to a train track and came out of the water. When I finally found out where I was, in Los Bonos, I collect called to Sammie at a friend's house, where she was waiting for my call; on hearing from me, she got so worried about me, that Cryxtal and Diamond completely escaped her mind. It was not until she was on the road, and halfway to pick me up, that she started to look for them, thinking they were in the backseat, and realized she had left them. Caught in between lover and children, Sammie chose me, because when you're special, you're special, and that's me—very special, especially in bed, that she can't get enough of. Leaving even her own mother for me, sometimes I thought that Sammie was a stupid bitch for following her heart, instead of her mind, which was fine with me, because I got to do whatever I wanted to do, and anytime that I felt like doing it, and that's what you call freedom from a lover; besides, people do what they're going to do anyway, no matter who said what. Anybody, when their mind is made up to do something, no one can stop 'em from what they wanted to do, and in Sammie's case, it was loving me.

CHAPTER 50

Ruth, Sammie's mother, had returned from Lowell; she couldn't take the silent treatment any longer, missing her daughter and grandchildren. Sammie's brother, Map, offered to assist, but Ruth would rather go through it by herself, because she wants the best for him, her son, and not to be a burden to him. Ruth talked him into staying with his nine-to-five job, and she caught the Amtrak; it's faster than the Hound, and the route is much easier, as it's just going straight. She stretched the miles across the United States, east to west, and got off the Amtrak alone in the Modesto station on Briggsmore. From here I don't know how this old lady did it. She doesn't speak a lick of English, didn't hardly know anyone in town, but managed to get herself around and into a house, with no job and with no credit. I don't know how she did it, but she found us at the river, with Diamond taking over the shopping cart in place of Cryxtal. He was asleep; Cryxtal and Sammie were by the river edge, building a sand castle, and I was on the old throwaway mattress, smoking chewy and crystal. The pipe was in my mouth, and the Bic lighter was going on high. At first glance, I didn't give a fuck; but on second look, I realized who it was, and it was already too late for me to put my shit to the side. But I tried to hide it anyway. Once I did, I lay back to watch 'em eyes on each other. How they both forgotten about everything and ran to each other's arms. Cryxtal was ankle deep inside the water, and she was crying, probably thinking that her mommy was running away from her, leaving her behind. I, too, got off my ass and raced to pick up Cryxtal. She was frightened. I tried to comfort her, but the bond between mother and daughter are stronger than ours; she wouldn't stop her crying. Refusing my comfort, pointing her cute little finger to where Sammie was with her mother, both of them still locked in one another's arms, crying on each other's shoulders, I felt guilty for Sammie as she chose to come looking for me and traded everything for this, all because of love. Ruth took Cryxtal from me; and she gently soothed her, running her fingers through Cryxtal's sticky hair, probably full of lice, getting it from Sammie, but everything was all right with Ruth. She was just happy that her only daughter was still alive, and for the first time, I experienced a scene of a mother's unconditional love, which I'll never have, and the meaning of what a mother's love stands for—a mother's love, a mother's love is unconditional. A mother will never abandon her child, outright will take a bullet for her baby; tough are mothers when it comes to love. Hollywood is different from the real stuff. Everything about a mother is trust. Running to a mother in time of stress, she will get you through, saving you out of your every trouble. Lovely, pleasing, and many other things is a mother. If only all children knew what a mother's love brings. Being very gentle and very soft is her thing. Ever and always, she will love you very much with her everything. And that's how a mother brings love, the kind of love that I never experienced, and I would never have known it if it wasn't for the relationship between Ruth and Sammie; but now I understand that some have it better than others, and there are others that have it worse than me. So the world is not a bad place, even though selfishness and envy and greed and all other unrighteous deeds are there.

CHAPTER 51

After Ruth cuddled everyone, I got a stare and a nod of the head from her for me to feel bad. I didn't hear one word from Ruth. Her silence had me wondering, maybe she understood that "if you don't have anything nice to say to someone, it is best if you don't say anything at all." But it didn't matter. I was just happy for mother and daughter and that they're together again; besides, it had been hell for Sammie since Ruth had been gone. I felt that I did more than enough of my share for her burden, and it was time for her to go back home to Lowell, but Sammie wouldn't go nowhere without me, leaving Ruth without a choice but to enlighten me on life; this was the first time that Ruth talked to me about responsibility and the future after Ruth put me in a position of no choice but to agree with her. Ruth booked a plane, paid the ticket, and we were on our way East. When we got to Boston Airport, Map, Sammie's brother, transported us back to Lowell, and Ruth gave me a fat Khmer-tradition wedding present. As quiet and undercover as Lowell was sleepy looking and depressing sometimes because of the snow, but at my wedding, the restaurant was packed—fifty-four tables, seats of ten. It was the moment I saw the same cheerful Sammie of old when I first met her. Map is my brother-in-law, so we're family now. Not satisfied with the last outcome of the business we had tried together, Map wanted to give it another try, and I was willing, but not to the point of trusting him with the 1.5 million capital that was needed. That was more than my everything, and I couldn't take any chance with my money; besides, I have children. I had myself and my children to think about, and the only reason why I still had the money was because I didn't know I had it till Mr. Cooper told me about it. Once again, I phoned Mr. Cooper because I saw what they saw—that is, we were family. But before I came to this commitment, I had everything set aside for my children, with a million put away with Mr. Cooper, potting it into earning. They should be all right with the interest alone. Watching my children play, with Sammie assisting them, for some reason my heart started to get heavy with misery; and when Map, Ruth, and Map's wife, Setha, with her baby girl, joined my Diamond and Cryxtal, I hated myself for coming into this beautiful family and destroying the good thing for them. But at the same time, I felt blessed to be a part of this happiness. Besides, Sammie chose me and made me a part of the family, and I thank God for that.

CHAPTER 52

After going over what Map had planned, this time I just demanded that 1.5 million be transferred into my new bank account at Fleet Bank from Mr. Cooper. I requested for both my savings and future money, leaving my estates money untouched, just in case things didn't work out, and like Chantho's words, "There's always a rainy day." I also requested that he contacts my U.S. Bank safe-deposit box, where I stashed my half of the key, in Stockton, to see if everything had been paid up-to-date. When Mr. Cooper got on the phone, I started out by thanking him, which was only right that I did. Mr. Cooper boomed in my ears, "Tommy, long time no hear from you, how you've been, and what happened to your car?" Car? How in the fuck did this motherfucker know about the car? So I told him everything.

"I'm sorry, Mr. Cooper, and you're the only person in this world that has been helping me, and I'm grateful for that. Thank you for everything, and after this, I'll try not to bother you no more." I did tell him, but the bottom line was that I really wanted to own my own used-car lot. He agreed to what we were talking about, but Mr. Cooper didn't follow through with my request though. I got mad; and once Mr. Cooper was on the line again when I called the second time, I let him had it, like I knew what the hell I was doing, and demanded for my money and for him to just do his job, but he came back at me with the nail hitting me on my head.

"If it wasn't for Kimberly, and Father Robert, you would be starving back in your country, and now you want to be mad and demand for your money, when I'm trying to look out for your best interest because of my words to my old friend. Well! Let me tell you this, Tommy Ok, how about I fix everything up, and make sure you don't get a penny out of Robert's wealth? So, from today on, Tommy, you continue with what you're doing, and don't call, and don't try to talk to me about money situation, because there is none for you, but beside the money, I do want you to call me once in a while to see how I'm doing, that would be nice of you." He told me this because he cared; I was stunned, and he was right, now I ended up with nothing. I brought the sad news to Map's attention; and he, too, was disappointed, thinking in the back of his head that I was lying to him. He thought that I didn't have enough confidence in his ability. But Mr. Cooper was right in not spoiling me, because if he would allow me, I would have wasted my wealth on a lost cause. Instead, he had Linda move my money into different stocks and buying options, or whatever the hell else that he was doing, but I did not know this was going on for my life. I felt like there was no reason for me to live on. I started to have thoughts about hanging myself off the bridge or the overpass, or just plain point-blank put a bullet to my head, and the only thing that kept me going was the dope; I had ran out of shit to smoke for two weeks already, and I was ready to return to Modesto, the capital of meth and supplier of the whole United States. The ache and pain between crack and joint, every part of me was calling for crystal. So I told Map and my mother-in-law, Ruth, and my wife, Sammie, that I was going back to Modesto to look for crystal in the same way that she was calling my name.

CHAPTER 53

There were tears in her eyes as she heard what came out of my mouth. Ruth tried to talk me out from going, but it didn't do any good; and when it was all said and done at the end, once again we left Map and his family behind and returned to Modesto, the home to the Hit Squad gang, where GTA are rated #1. I don't know what it is, but there's just something about Modesto that has so much meaning to me. I guess because Modesto is a beautiful city that treated me badly; when my heart desired happiness, it filled me up with sadness. I wanted freedom, but I only had shackles and chains. I found my love but only to be left behind. I was locked up and almost didn't have a chance to get out; on the street, my life was put under supervision, not to leave the Central Valley more than fifty miles out of town. Sometimes I wonder why Modesto treated me with so many conditions, leaving me to run into problems and troubles, with no lead way; except the drugs and brews and E & J Gallo had me confused between two worlds, reality and imagination, lost in the gangland on the Westside, getting my dick sucked by fiends and prostitutes. When I lost all my integrity and did the wrong thing, the authority put me in jail, sending me off to prison without rehabilitation, only to be released back to my addiction, one that I didn't know how to overcome. Opportunities were there, but for me there were none. I went on the run and found out that I was standing up against something that was too powerful. I forced myself to try and make the same mistakes, ending up in the same cell. Many times I reached out for help, but aid never came; even friends outside couldn't do anything for my situation. I had no family, no friends, no one to depend on; and this time around, I questioned myself, "What does it take to live in Modesto?" The more I thought about it, the more I didn't know what to do. I've tried moving away, close and far, only to find myself desiring and craving for more of Modesto; and before long, once again I was back to the same ghetto, and with more trouble. It was like there was no way out. I needed help to find my way, for Modesto to stop treating me in such a way. My interests were to live right and raise a family, but at the same time, so were the chances of sitting in prison for life without parole, with the new three strikes law and all. But with crystal on my mind, I had room for nothing else; and as soon as we were off the Amtrak and checked in at the Traveller's Inn, I called up Lice, and I headed out to the connection house. I didn't play around and was serious about my drug smoking. Grabbing me an ounce and stopping at the Rock Shop to grab a couple of glass-bubble pipes, I was ready to party, going back to my old life. I didn't finish my tweeking until a week passed; and when I came back to the motel, Ruth, Sammie, and the children had already checked out. The first thing that came to my mind was that she was going back to Lowell. Oh, how wrong I was, so I went on with my addiction and activity, living in the fast lane that only in America exists.

CHAPTER 54

Meanwhile Sara Long was carrying a child, and her quick, blooming relationship had started to slowly die out. But from the abortion experience with my child, she dared not do such an abomination and decided to keep the child. She and her man had purchased a house together; and now her man was gone, leaving her with all the bills, payments, and the whole liabilities. She had to work two jobs to keep up with things. As her belly was getting bigger, she was also having a hard time moving around. So she quit one of her jobs and had her car for repo; next in line was the house. So she went back to the grandparents after the bank repossessed the house. I knew I should be thrilled and be filled with joy at her ill fate; but for whatever reason, I felt sorry for her, that all these were happening to her. I didn't know why, I just knew that she deserved better; and if she knew about my money, things between us probably wouldn't be like this, because besides Sammie, everybody else that I ran into was all about the money. Money is everything to everyone, but then again, I couldn't take somebody else's problems and make it into my personal shit. And to me, Sara brought all that shit upon herself. If only she had stayed true to me through thick and thin, I would have done as I had promised her, making sure she does not have to do anything, only stay home, watch the children, and go shopping. But she didn't think that I was capable, and to the point of calling me a loser, when her monthly income was only a couple of cents compared to my assets. I have to say, Sara Long is a dumb-ass bitch, one that traded temporary pleasures for long term of the easy and relaxed lifestyle. Oh well, that's on her. But we came together again when I was sitting in prison; with both Ruth and Sammie dead in a car accident, that made room for us for another try. But like all things in life, once something went wrong, it can never be right again, no matter how you try to fix it or how much time you put in. It would never be the same again, and this is one of those cases between me and your mother, Sara Long. Sometimes I wish things would work out. I have to admit, I wanted to care for her, be her husband. I guess my love for her is to no end, or maybe she's my heaven sent, and the man in me is separating what God had joined together.

CHAPTER 55

My smoking habit had come back to full swing, blowing big clouds and forgetting everything, with me not able to find my mother-in-law and family (I mean, not that I tried hard), because they were only living on Fourth Street, on J between Third, next to the alley behind AM/PM. Sammie went to Paradise looking for me, doing it maybe out of love or the need to smoke some shit herself that she was looking for me, and when she did, she found me on the upstairs apartment at Sally's place. She was nothing like that dumb-ass Sara, who thinks her shits don't stink. Sammie didn't talk shit or said anything. All she did was smile and make her way to where I was sitting on the sofa with a smile. She took a seat next to me and looked around to make sure that no ears were in sound sight and whispered, "Can I talk to you, outside?" I got up and followed her. Before anything, she told me, "I miss you, Tommy," and the way she made it sound got tears forming in my eyes, chocking all my words, leaving me speechless with only my arms alive to wrap her in, only to run around, leaving her chasing after me like a game of cat and butterfly. From here to there, no matter where I go, Sammie would be on my tail, from one hotel to the next motel; in town or out, she would not stop, and every chance, I made time for her. It was always paradise for her—no, not 620 Paradise, because that's me, going from house to house, place after place, always on the go, nonstop, until I was forced into the basement. Under my mother-in-law's house, I started to turn my tweeking into something positive; I started to go through the encyclopedia, adding knowledge to my learning. I would stay down in the basement for days, sometimes even forgetting if it was daylight or night. The only time I left out of the basement was to go to the connection house, and sometimes, not even that, they'll bring the drug to me. Sammie had slowed down and been thinking of quitting altogether and started to hate me for smoking that shit, killing myself, but she would say, "It's better he smoke here, alone where I can be close to him, and smoke, than smoke elsewhere and not know what could happen." Ruth's words with me began to decline, and within just a couple of months, it went silent altogether, and that's how we lived our lives 'til the day I got arrested. And we never had the chance to say good-bye to each other. I guess you can say she was a good mother-in-law, and a good grandma too, always busying herself with both Cryxtal and Diamond, bending herself for what they want, to make sure that her grandchildren had what they needed—milk and bottle, diaper and clothing, shoes, and funds for fun places. Most of all, Ruth was always there for the family, and never one time did she complain.

CHAPTER 56

After I was sick of the encyclopedia, Hitler, and Ruth, I started to go out again, this time to make things easier for myself, with Sammie stuck at home with the baby. I would only come home to drop Sammie off some dope, new pipes, pick up my Cryxtal and Diamond to kiss them real quick and drop them back down as fast, and out the door again. Leaving the three of them to cry after me, I was too numb to have any feelings for her. It went from every other day, to every week, and into months sometimes before I came home. Using up all my funds in my bank account, now it was hard for me to move around. I used what knowledge Sammie had taught me. I turned it into a crime. It paid for a while, but like all crime, it didn't pay for long—not for my straight-A friends nor the salesman Scott Peterson—but I was in too deep and felt it was too late to pull myself out or turn around from the wrong road I was taking. I would only come home to eat and sleep; and when Sammie got me a cell phone, she would call me nonstop, so I would trade it off for some shit, because I knew that the minute I sold it, I could call Sammie and tell her to disconnect the service. And a couple of times, I even managed to receive refund checks for her, as I kept on stacking the payments in advance for the service up to a year's payment by a friend; and once the service was disconnected, the company has to reimburse the money, and it worked all the time. It wasn't a gain of a million-dollar plan, but it was enough to get by during my smoking era. Talking about phones, I remember one time, I was trying to get a phone hooked up under someone else's profile, and I wasn't approved, so I told the operator, "Fuck you," after she told me that my credit wasn't good enough. I got into telling the girl that I had a lot of things on my mind and that I had chosen the company with the hope of having a chance to establishing my credit, and the girl bought my story and hooked up the phone for me, but not for long though, as the phone got traded or sold for some shit. It seemed like I couldn't gather enough crystal; it was like the more I buy, the lesser I have, to the point of doing anything and everything like the dope fiend that I vowed long ago not to become one. Down to 119, and with every hit of the pipe, my stomach hurt, as I haven't eaten for too long and drank for many days, and no sleep for many nights didn't help. When I do sleep, I would sleep a whole week straight at a time, only get up to eat the food that Sammie brought to me in bed, which was not far from the fridge. Yes! I slept on the kitchen floor on a little thin mattress. The kitchen was my bedroom, and my living room was the patio out back, where I smoked and did all my stupid shit out in the open. I missed fucking with my fighting roosters. He was a baby champ. I had to go all the way to Porterville to get it from the Hmong people, but too bad, the young stag never had a chance to see the rink, because I had him on a tight cord because of the living spaces in the small backyard, and the stupid chicken decided to go over the fence and got himself caught in between falloff as he tried to learn how to crow. He got hang upside down to his death like Peter on the cross. I was heated when I came home and found it dead; I cut the rope and tossed the cock into the trash and put the fire to his end.

CHAPTER 57

One time, I almost lost myself. I was so fucked up that day, that I started to see things that weren't there and hear things when there was no sound. I was into roosters at the time, and I will never forget the hallucination. My mind flipped and took me there. I started to trip hard, beginning to see roosters everywhere that I turned. I saw one on top of the wooden fence of my connection house, when there was no chicken there; I shook that thought out of my head, telling myself I was fucked up, and as we came to a stop sign, it happened again. I looked at the doghouse, there was a rooster perching on top of it, and then the whole world started to flip on me. Now trash cans were turning to round cages. It was crazy, and things got even crazier when we heard the news about the owner of the house that we were renting from being dead. This eighty-two-year-old man's face was everywhere I went, and everywhere I looked, I saw his face. He was smiling at me with the smile of his picture that was on top of the casket. I couldn't run, I couldn't hide; there was no escaping, his face was everywhere. Even the weed that I smoked to calm me down and to put me to sleep didn't help, and as I was going insane by myself, Sammie wanted to send me to a rehab. "Honey! You don't have to go on or keep on doing this to yourself, rehab can help," Sammie said.

"You fuckin' stupid bitch! Don't you fuckin' know that a motherfucker like me is on the run?" I busted out in fury, and Sammie was so blind to love that she stayed silent. I called up my newfound smoker crimie, Steve B. Welch, a bulky white guy. His dad picked up the phone every time I called since I met him. We had plans, but I acted like we were going fishing, and Sammie caught on. As soon as I was out the door, Sammie probably thought to herself, *I would do what others don't*. And that was to stay loving Tommy Ok no matter what. She had a couple of espionages of her own, the motherfuckin' haters who spied on me and reported my whereabouts, my activity, and who I was with, and so on. She didn't find me at first, as only a few chosen ones would know where I was at. I was at the little glowing blue motel in Ripon. I was talking about cuts with no one expecting someone like my self to be in, but for some reason, Sammie caught up on me.

I was partying, when there was a knock on the door; one of the girls went to lower the music down, and it came, "Open up, punk! I know you're in there." On hearing the voice, it was my Sammie, but the language that was being used was not hers. Inside was me, Steve B. Welch, and four other bitches; we were waiting for Mondough to show up, and he was always lagging, forever running late. One of the bitches was kind of my regular—half black, half white, she looked all right, and I loved the way she sucked. She was a professional; when I was in her butt, she knew how to work her muscles around the hole. I tell you, she ain't no joke or just an ordinary prostitute off the street. She knows how to make you hot, burn, and melt you down like ice. The replica came again, "Open up, punk! I know you're in there."

I told Steve B. Welch, "Get all the girls into the back room." There were panicked looks on the two Asian girls' faces, because they knew that females take their men seriously—a Hmong, and one Laos; and the Mexican girl, she was not too bad looking, with silky and straight jet-black hair, and Steve B. Welch was dying to get into that pussy. But little did he know that she was my old hoe that I threw away, but we were still friends for rainy days; besides, who can forget memories of the car, the open field, the park, on the road, off the road, in the bathroom, near the water—we had done it all, that's why we can't let each other go, but at the same time, it ain't no fun if the homie can't have none. And that's how we do it out here in Modesto, smoke dope and fuck for fun.

Chapter 58

My heart will always belong to my wife, Sammie; no matter what I do, or who I'm doing it with, it will not be the same as me and Sammie, because our love is special, and who could ask for more than a noble wife like her? From the way she was knocking on the door, I knew she was heated. I went to the peephole and couldn't believe my eyes, as I saw my wife standing there in shorts with a purse in one hand and a key chain in the other. I had to think quick; first things first, I got all the girls to hurry up and get dressed. I told them, "My wife is outside. Go to the other room and go hide in the bathroom, while I take care of my baby mama." Fuck! I was saying to myself out loud. Opening the door, I tried to give her my little innocent-boy smile and reached out to take a hold of her, trying to kiss ass, but she just busted the door open, moving past me and storming inside.

On seeing the room empty, she ordered, "Everybody can come out now." But she didn't dare to go around searching the hotel, so she turned to order me to do it, "Bring all your little bitches out," and she finish with, "I know they're in here, I can smell them."

"Come on, baby," I pleaded, and I thought by now she knew better—that the only time I used the word "baby" was when I had something to hide or was not telling the truth about something. "I ain't got nobody in here beside Steve B. Welch. We were trying to program some shit, trying to make some money," I told her.

"Bullshit! I don't believe you unless you're telling me you're fucking each other." She accused Steve B. Welch as he tried to help me out on hearing this. The motherfucker turned into one of the bitches and went to hide with them. My mind was on all the possibilities of how he might hate me and tip me off to my baby momma. One of the stupid bitches, Pamala, had to come out; and as soon as Sammie saw her, her eyes got big, and she screamed at me, "You see! I knew you wasn't just here playing with each other, and the laptop. Who the fuck is this bitch anyway? What, my pussy not good enough for you, that you have to sneak around behind my back?" I tried to fit Pamala into matching her with Steve B. Welch, but I knew Sammie wouldn't buy it.

So I turned to myself, "Fuck! Fuck!" Frustrated, I just threw myself onto the bed and called for everybody to come on out; and as Sammie was standing by the door, probably ready to run, nervous that something might happen, I introduced her, "Everyone this is my wife Sammie."

"What the fuck, Tommy? Don't tell me that you fucked all these girls at the same time?" she barked. And she waited for my answer, but I have long learned not to give one. She said, "You're in trouble to one, all you bitches gonna get it." When she got no answer from me nor any response from any of the bitches, like always she took it out on everybody else and not her lover Tommy. Never him; he can never be at fault in her eyes. Always a perfect angel, no matter how filthy I was, I was pure and clean.

Chapter 59

Man, out of nowhere, Sammie started to sling on Pamala, who was the closest to her; just as I looked up, I saw Pamala drop to the ground, holding the side of her face where she got punched. I was like what the fuck, as I had never seen that side of Sammie before. The three girls were backing up upon witnessing what had happened to their friend. And before one of the girls could turn, Sammie grabbed Kathy by the back of her head and pulled her down to the ground with both her legs going up in the air, exposing her pussy; Sammie was kicking her now, saying, "You want to fuck with my dick? Ha! Bitch!" I was thinking to myself, *I gotta get out of there. This bitch has turned savage overnight.* Making a run across the room to the car that Steve B. Welch took from his parents, I raced out the door, with Steve B. Welch right behind my tail. Then came Sammie, running and yelling, "Come back, Tommy! If you don't, I'm going to call the cops."

On hearing this, I yelled back, "You'll never see me again"

"Okay! Stop! I won't call the pig on you. I love you, Tommy," she cried. "Tommy! Baby! Please don't go. Wait for me. I'm not going to call no police, just stop, and talk to me." But I only stopped to look at her and tossed Steve B. Welch his parents' car key. I told him to bring it around the corner and pick me up. He did, my breathing so hard, and we drove off in silence, looking through the rearview mirror. I could see that my Sammie was crying; but I couldn't bring myself to tell Steve B. Welch to stop or turn back, and that was all I had to do, but I didn't, leaving her to cry and go back home full of tears and her heart heavy with deep disappointment. When she walked in the house to her Diamond and Cryxtal, she felt sorry for her children, plus a little for herself, but especially Cryxtal. In the cold, with the sky as her rooftop from birth, she had to experience what toddlers don't normally go through; and also Sammie was crying for herself, as she didn't understand and was confused of her love for me, not wanting her mother to see her sorrow. She picked up both Cryxtal and Diamond and went to the bathroom to cry a little more of her sadness out and to wash her face, to try and hide the truth, but Ruth already knew. It was just that she couldn't do nothing about it. Besides, parents are like God; they know even your shit. So there's nothing we can conceal from them. Like the good mother that she was, Ruth understood with a sad heart Sammie's love for Tommy, and she was mad at herself that there was nothing that she could do to help her child with her problems. So she did the best thing, and that was to stay quiet, not saying anything, bad or good. She only stayed close to support and lived up to her responsibilities as a mother, and to love her children unconditionally, because that's what being a mother is all about. Ruth understood her position and stayed out of Sammie's way.

CHAPTER 60

Steve B. Welch, out of nowhere, burst out laughing to himself during the drive, like he was Mad Dogg. So I asked him, "What the fuck, fool!" But he kept laughing, and it took him a minute to control himself.

"Man! Your baby mamma is fuckin' crazy. I've never seen anything like this before, it's better than movie, man!" he said with some excitement. "Not even in a movie you'll see action like this," he conceded. "Your girl is dope, man." And he complimented, "You hella lucky to have a girl to love you the way that your baby mamma do." In lots of ways, I was the luckiest guy in the whole planet to have Sammie. On replaying the events in my head, I myself started to burst out laughing; when I saw the way she was standing with both hands on her hips, she looked a little like Mona—the face that she had, and how she manhandled them bitches. After the laughters came the tears of worry. "Fool! What do you think is happening back there right now?" Steve B. Welch asked.

"How the hell I'm supposed to know when I'm here with you?" I answered him with a question. "You sure you're not crossing me? Uh! I know what it is, you are trying to get me and my wife to fight, so we can be separated, and you can move in." *Rrr!*

"Come on, Flea, you know I have too much respect for you to do something like that," he tried to plead, only to have me question him if he knew anything about the Bible.

"Do you know anything about the Bible?" I asked. When he nodded yes, I continued, "Well! Then you should know about King David. Because of love, he killed his best friend for his wife."

"I can't believe you can even start thinking like that about me," Steve B. Welch tried to bail himself out. "I take Sammie as my sister, Flea, and your children are my godchildren."

"If you don't want me to feel this way about you, so why did you lie to me?" I pushed him.

"I didn't, Flea, the only person I called was Mondough, and he was supposed to show up, and it happened to be your baby mamma instead." Hmmm! Some shit was not right, and it was hard to figure out; because Steve B. Welch didn't do it, then it had gotta be Mondough. And sure enough, when the truth came out, it was his punk azz who had been hating me. No wonder no matter where I went, Sammie seemed to be able to track me down, and to this day, I wonder what else they got going. And if they were fucking or not, the truth will never come out, because Sammie already took it to the grave with her.

CHAPTER 61

When I came in the know and was for sure that it was my enemy within Mondough, I warned Steve B. Welch to watch out for that fool! Out of madness because of the betrayal, I told Steve B. Welch to take me to the connection house and grabbed myself an ounce of crystal, and with enough money for gas to go out of town, we went to pick up Mondough. From his place, he seemed to know what he did, feeling guilty, and didn't want to come along at first; then on second thought, as he saw all the dope I was flashing, his mind flipped, and going against his better judgment, he hopped in the car with us. Cruising out of town, in my fury I could have easily snapped him in half, which brought me to see that everybody in America is a victim of all sorts—victim of love, of war on the streets, of drugs across the country, for race, colors, beliefs, success, failure, freedom, and liberty, and no matter who you are, you are a victim of something. Even the very judge that has the power and authority to send people to prison is a human just like everybody else, born the same way, came out equipped with the same things (arms, legs, body, head, and brain); we all get blessed the same, but why does all fate fall on one and not the other? Why are there bums and the world's richest man, Bill Gates? And here I am, smoking dope, doing no good for anyone, not even myself, destroying my physical being; and that's bad, very bad, because my body is all I have to cover my whole being, keeping everything inside, hiding my deepest and darkest secret, and keeping my pain and fears hidden from the naked eyes—where my heart is protected and my head full of brains rests. When I'm hurt and alone, my feelings and emotions comfort me. And look, what do I do for my body in render? Years later, as I turned back through time, I see that I, too, am a man, and I don't have superpowers to overcome the very things that are too strong for others; and for thinking that I'm stronger, better, and able to contain anything, to the point of never losing my freedom to anything, looking into the past I saw I was wrong, not as strong, and had paid dearly for my mistakes. And like all mistakes, I lived up to the repercussions, and I endured all weaknesses like all human beings do, plus some extra—a little more through hard times and being in hostile environments, where only the strong survived and the weak got their body taken.

CHAPTER 62

Going northbound, Steve B. Welch took the Fremont exit in Stockton, made the first right, then a left turn into a trailer park. We were going to see a biker that Steve B. Welch knew from when they were in the service together; on setting my eyes on this monster, he looked all dusty and disgusting, filthy, with long hair, and his breath was the Rocky Mountains course factory. That shit was brewing. We went to the backyard and into a medium-size shake, where we would be in for two days and two nights smoking, tweaking bikes and trying to program phones. Mondough was lovin' all the dope, and he was now tweeking off to himself. He had been at the same spot for I don't know how long, playing a hold 'em poker game. Steve B. Welch and I weren't any help to the biker; I think his name is Big John Stud. I myself didn't know nothing about bikes, but I was sure taking it apart, and the next thing you know, his bike sat empty. He was like, what the fuck, but on second thought, he said it good, "Now I can start fresh from nothing."

I told him, "Hey, man! Sorry about your bike, I'm on a good one, that's why."

"Yeah, your shit is heavy duty." I had enough of this tweeking shit and was ready to come home to my Sammie. Cleaning my hands, I watched Steve B. Welch showing off his work to his old marine buddy and Jimmy—oh yeah, that was what his name was, Big Jim. He tried to start the bike that Steve B. Welch had just put together, turning the key, but I didn't hear nothing, no engine sound nor nothing. So Big Jim reached over and grabbed the cigarettes that sat on top of the gas tank, and the damn bike got caught on fire on its own. Big Jim didn't even light up the cigarette, or at least according to his story. But the whole bike was up in smoke. Lucky it didn't explode. Not waiting around to find out the cause—I was on the run as it was, and I wanted to get away from any scene that will attack the police—I signaled to Steve B. Welch, pointing to the car with my index finger. Mondough, who was still stuck inside the shack, didn't even know what just happened. We got in the car and honked for his stupid ass to come out the shack so we can bounce, but he didn't come out, so we could not bounce; the motherfucker was too far gone and didn't even hear us honking. He was on a damn good one. So I told Steve B. Welch to run in and pull his punk ass out so that we can cut out; once he got Mondough's ass in the car, we headed out, cutting across downtown from 99 to I-5. Still going northbound, we stopped at Anderson, at a remote place. We pulled over; me and Steve B. Welch could have done Mondough in, but I had already had my share of bloodbath. And I just wanted to know the truth of why he was CIA-ing on me, and when I came to find out, it was Sammie who had been putting the pressure on him; and his truth was, "You know how I am, when I'm on one." Thinking about it, it was true; he had been turning into a pussy when he was on one. So I let everything be the way it was and blamed Steve B. Welch. "What the hell, fool! Why the fuck you bring me all the way up here for?"

"You said to just drive, and that's all I'm doing," Steve B. Welch answered.

"Well, just get back on the freeway and take me home." On the way back, I passed out, as I haven't slept for weeks already. Mondough woke me up to take a hit, but that, too, didn't help, as my eyes refused to be cracked open and stayed locked shut like each other.

CHAPTER 63

Coming down hard, I didn't even need the weed to relax me or calm me down. When I started to feel like this, I knew it was time to go home, wash up, get into a set of new clothing, and sleep, lots of sleep; and whenever I was sleeping, Sammie wouldn't allow no one to disturb my rest—not even the U.S. president is important enough to wake me from my sleep. Sitting in the car, my body was exhausted, feeling all dry, drained out of water, but my eyes wouldn't catch no sleep after the hit I took. Fuck it! I rolled up a blunt and took the whole shit to my head; that, too, didn't help. I was about to revive myself with a quick power nap, since I was already hella tired, and my body already ached. I was ready to rest my neck, and I was out cold with my neck hanging. First things first, and that was the shower, then brush my teeth, because my breath smelled like do-do; Father Robert used to tell me, "So you better take care of your inside first then the outside, your head, and work your way down, rinse and you're all fresh and clean, and ready for the day." Stepping out of the shower, Sammie came with a warm towel that she had thrown into the dryer for me. She didn't bother to let me dry off my own self. And like she was my slave, she worked my wet body with the towel and my dripping prick with her warm mouth. I needed to use the bathroom, needed to take a shit, so I moved to sit on the toilet; at the same time, Sammie couldn't let go of what she was sucking on to. She continued to give me head while I shit. I don't recall feeling anything out of the ordinary when she sucked my dick while shit came out my asshole. Besides smelling like shit, I guess you can say, it's the little things like this that makes life interesting and adds fun to relationships. Once I was dry, both my body and my sperm, she treated me the same as she did to Cryxtal and Diamond, putting my clothes on for me. I was the king, and as she pulled my boxer up, she didn't pull it all the way up but let it hang at the kneecaps. Taking her time, she gently stroked my cock and brought her mouth to choke on it, munching it, and letting it hit the back of her throat, making me nut in her mouth, and she swallowed all of it, like the "sperm sponge" that she told me she was. Once my load was released, my whole body went weak, and I couldn't stand on my own. Sammie had to hold on to my legs to keep me from falling, with her mouth still glued to my cock. I was swinging from side to side, like a tree being moved by the wind very gently from side to side. After she finished dressing me up, I went to bed, and Sammie went to the kitchen to bring me one of the many foods she had prepared for me. I was almost out when Sammie walked in with the tray of overflowing food, and while I ate, she went out and brought in Diamond and Cryxtal to spend whatever time I had before I passed out. I ate, fed my children, and played with them a little. When I had my full, it was time for me to pass out; sometimes I woke up to Sammie working the dick, or on top of me, enjoying herself, by herself, while I was out cold for weeks at a time.

CHAPTER 64

Sara Long was about to be due, and she will have to go through the labor on her own. I was so strung out that I didn't make it to the delivery room for the birth of Alexandria. So what makes anyone think that I'm going to be there for someone else's baby? Besides, that's someone else's responsibility. So alone, she had the baby. At least it was better than Brenda, who had her baby in the bathroom. It was a cute little curly haired half-black baby boy, and Sara named him Johnathan. Even though we didn't live far from each other, I didn't even have time to go see my daughter or the newborn. With each passing day, I fell deeper into self-destruction, and it was almost complete. I know myself, that if I don't take hold of myself now, I might never have a chance. I went over what I have done, to try and overcome the drug. I ran away to Lowell, Massachusetts, from the East Coast to up North, Washington State, and everywhere else in between, I tried to get myself clean, but I always found myself back in Modesto, smoking again and again, with no escape, leaving me with only one option. And that was to keep on smoking; then I came to myself one day—since I was already on the run, I figured I can take care of two problems at one shot. By now, from being in and out of jail, I pretty much knew what crime carried what sentence before I was incarcerated. I evaluated the time frame with the crime that will fit the time I needed to overcome it. I was doing the wrong thing on purpose, trying to earn my pass to go to prison; before I got arrested, I told all my so-called friends—or I should say my smoking, tweeking peers—that the time I was sitting in jail will be the time that I will make the most money in my life. At the time I made this statement, I really didn't know what I was talking about myself; and when I finally did sit in jail and remembered what came out of my mouth about me making the most money in my life, that was when I knew I had to prove myself right and everyone else wrong, including Mondough, who thought I told on him when

I was the one who was doing everybody's time. I had reason to feel bad for having to carry everybody else's load; but then again, if you want to hold the sword like Lion-O in the ThunderCats, you have to endure more than the rest. Besides, I'm the better man, and without the black and white, who can say anything about a motherfucker like me?

CHAPTER 65

Sammie was so nice; she was the only girl that I had ever heard thanking me for a good fuck. All the other ones, never, not even Sara Long whom I made nut like no other man before. She never thanked me for the best fuck that I gave her. Midway into my drug-abuse problem, I came to a point where I just wanted to stay home and get high. But I couldn't do that because the damn drug cost too much, and I didn't want to do any of my illegal activities around the house because I'm scared of the CPS (Child Protective Service). And from what my instinct told me, every day I woke up with the feeling of being watched and followed around, but I didn't give a fuck because I already knew sooner or later I was going to be sitting in jail. I got up quickly at any hours, and before the shower was the glass pipe; as soon as I cracked my eyes open, I hit the pipe. Sammie, who was now drug free, still loaded it up and melted it down for me. One time I was still sleeping, and a special friend Chancy came to visit, woke me up to hit the pipe after he melt it down. It was still liquid and boiling hot as I reached over to grab the GP from his hand. The crystal dripped out of the airhole when I accidentally turned the pipe upside down without knowing, and I got burned. I got hotly mad, and I smoked till I got my energy back before I hopped in the water, got dressed, and out the door to repeat the same thing over again. Going around, rounding up the people that I felt could help me get my hand on some crystal and had IDs to rent a motel for me to use, I was trying anything that I could think of that could bring in money or generate income from the computer, to check fraud, and different other things, including mail. The good thing about a tweeker's crime though, most of the time, they are nonviolent and non-life threatening; well, besides when shit blows up, trying to cook up some shit. Other than that, tweekers tend to stay away from people and the public, always hiding out during the day and coming out only at night, like some kind of night creatures. This time, we were chilling at Motel 6. It was

Steve B. Welch, Mondough, and six other bitches. We were partying, having a good time, getting in the move to do a gangbang group sex, and were having a one-of-a-kind fun. But the next thing you know, my fuckin' baby momma again; the knock came first, then, "Come on out, you punk! I know you're in there."

Without a doubt, I knew it was my love, Sammie; and in my madness, not of Sammie's action, but because of the hater, I went out and demanded, "Who the fuck been working for you and told you where I'm at?"

Her response was, "No one, I followed you myself."

"And how long have you been doing this?" I conceded.

"Don't worry, that's for me to know and for you to find out."

I had no comeback for her remark, and with that, I stormed back into the room and told Steve B. Welch, "Hey, fool! When I go out to talk to my wife, you sneak out, get the car and bring it around, and I'll jump in and we take off. She's been following me, HA!" Going back out to face Sammie, I softly asked her, "Baby! Why are you following me for?"

"Because I love you," she answered with no hesitation.

"I love you too, that's why you can't be on me like fly on shit."

"Well, take me along with you, like how you used to back then, everywhere with you." And I remembered the three of us, with Diamond still in her stomach. I knew I should've gone home with her, but I was too blind to see anything beyond the crystal; and the higher I got, the more my life lived by deceit, hiding behind the substance that I almost died because of it.

CHAPTER 66

Let me not overexaggerate on how I have come to make some money by doing the wrong things and breaking the law. But as a dad, I thought of my children's future, and I tried to start up Cryxtal's and Diamond's savings accounts, but when I brought it to Sammie's attention, she reassured me, "Tommy! I don't need for you to do anything to get the money for our children. Legal or illegal, I already have everything laid out for both of them. I just want you home." She lowered her voice. "Honey, I love you and I miss the old you, before the drug. You worry me sick every time you're away. That's why I choose to come looking for you because I care. I don't want you—" Before she could finish off her word, I started to move toward the bin, as I spotted Steve B. Welch coming around the corner. I quickly sprinted and hopped in the car, and we were gone, with me yelling out, "I love you, go home."

"Come back, Tommy."

And the only thing that came to her was, "I'm sorry, I'll see you at home."

"When?" Sammie cried out in desperation. That was the last word that I heard from Sammie's mouth, till I collect called to her from the county jail, for receiving stolen property. Getting on 99 South, we were on our way out to Merced. Steve B. Welch had some stolen checks, and we were looking for someone to cash it, but we found no one in Modesto or Merced to do it; that got us to lose hope and decide to abandon the plan of going all the way to Bakersfield. Cashing checks coming home, we stopped at Delhi, the town where I burned myself almost to death trying to cook dope and got myself burned bad. We stopped by the grapevine that can be seen from the freeway, and we got our smoke on. Inside the car, there was a backpack, a typewriter, and other papers of profiles that Steve B. Welch was supposed to drop off at the house of a friend of his, but he didn't locate the friend.

On coming back on 99 North, Steve B. Welch was mashing, going fast, trying to catch up with the speed that we just smoked, and got the light turned on us for us to be pulled over, but I told him, "Don't stop, keep going." The siren was sounded, which was the warning that we needed to do a high-speed chase; we did good, doing 125-130 MPH on the freeway, 'til we exited and ran into a dead end, hitting the fence and a parked car. That blacked me out, and the cop beat me up pretty badly. They broke my collarbone; I had to be taken to the hospital and out of all the things that they did, to treat my wound, draw my blood for tests of drug and alcohol levels. After the hospital, and the treatment that I didn't get, I was being transferred to Ceres PD for questioning and interrogation, but I told them to talk to my public defender when I was questioned by the officers. So they left me alone and in a lot of pain; I was thrown into one of the daytime cruisers after shift change and was transferred to the Stanislaus County Jail, with a $55,000 bail. That might not be a lot of money to some people, but to a tweeker like me and my welfare family, it was a lot of money, but not enough to stop Sammie from bailing me out.

CHAPTER 67

Going through the booking process, in the holding tank, I placed a call to Sammie and broke the news to her. "Baby! I'm in jail, my bail is set at $55,000." I went on as she stayed in silence, probably trying to recover from her shock. "Can you bail me out?" I pleaded.

"How?" was her question.

"I don't know," I told her, but I gave her my good friend Woody's number, and for her to give him a call. He'll be able to help me get out of this hellhole, and if he can't do it, contact Leroy. I don't know how she pulled off this miracle, but she was able to come up with the 10 percent of $55,000; and with Mr. Woody, who I knew would come through like how he did for many people many times before, once again he came through. Thanks Mr. Woody!

Two hours later, I was being called out of the M-tank and was told, "You're bailed out." A convict asked me my name and came back with a netted bag and threw me my street clothes from where they stored all personal belongings on the second floor. Mr. Woody was out front in the visiting lobby waiting for me. The door clicked, the officer pushed the heavy metal door open, and with a smart remark, he bid his "good-bye, visit again soon, punk motherfucker."

Woody walked me across the street, took me into his office right across from the main downtown jail about a block away to sign some papers, and as we were done and turning to leave, he reminded me, "Your court date is December 11."

"Okay," I replied. "Thanks," and I was out the door, waiting outside for him to give me a ride home.

When we got to the house, Sammie ran into my arm, and after the hugs and kisses, she told me, "We only had 5 percent of the bail."

In my puzzlement I asked, "So how did you bail me out?" And right away, my mind was telling me, *My wife loves me enough to get fucked by another man just to get me out?* I quickly shook this stupid idea out of my head.

On seeing the confusion on my face, Sammie said, "I persuaded him."

And what a relief; I can only manage to let out, "Oh!" Now I had another problem on my hand. How was I going to come up with the other 5 percent of the money, as Sammie agreed to a thirty-day same-as-cash deal? I thought about the possibility of how I can make some money or come up with it, what I have to do, etc., but really, I didn't have to come up with no money because Sammie already had the finances in place for everything. When her father Paul passed away, he had a life insurance. And since Sammie was his favorite, everything went to her, but since she didn't say anything about it, I didn't know nothing about it and kept on going with my destructive way of living; and that was what Sammie was worried about, that I might use the money to kill myself, smoking dope to my death. So she did the best thing by hiding her riches from me. I was not running from the law no more, but a couple of days later, I was picked up by the U.S. Marshals and got transferred back to Oklahoma. They let me off the hook with a slap on my hand; again, on my own, I wanted to stay back a bit, hang around Lawton, and visit people I haven't seen in a long while. But Sammie was ahead of me and had already bought me a plane ticket and was ready to pick me up at the San Francisco Airport to take me back to Modesto, my home and my town that I have grown to appreciate in more ways than one, both good and bad ones.

CHAPTER 68

I didn't waste no time in getting back to my habit that I was powerless under. As soon as I stepped foot on Modesto Street, Sammie already had everything set up for me. From the men's room, I got my smoke on inside the airport lobby, and all the way home, backseat smoking in the car, plus some more once inside the house; by this time, with every hit I took, my well-maintained body was starting to take its toll. From the too many years of not eating right and not sleeping properly, every time I took a hit by then, my kidney ached. I knew I had to do something with my abuse problem. I needed a solution fast, or something terrible was going to happen to my physical being. The addiction was so strong that I could not stop smoking and snorting lines and now moving to needles, starting to build tracks on my arm—something that I didn't dare to try before—and I was doing the unthinkable. My nose started to get messed up a little as I got nosebleeds, and so were my teeth, from all those years of grinding them together. I even at times found it hard to breathe, and if I kept on going at this rate that I was going, the only place I'd end up would be six feet underground, and that couldn't happen, because I had big dreams and desired to do great things. It hadn't been all that great for me so far, but the wick of my hope hadn't all completely went out; and all I had to do was add oil to it to keep the flame going, but if I didn't do something about it by then, I might not have a chance. I went over my own life, trying to search for the power that I needed to overcome my addiction. I was without any ID, social security card, and on top of that, I was on bail, which made matters that much harder for me, as I couldn't relocate anywhere. Already I knew that prison is "the refuge city" for someone as myself, but I wasn't in no hurry to go there and get saved; besides, you just can't walk in to prison and say you want to do time or take refuge. The only way to make it in to prison is to get involved with criminal and illegal activities, which I took part of and joined hands with, doing my share, getting caught up for some bullshit, getting charged with GTA when I was on the passenger side. It was crazy for me, how I was charged. I was in full confusion, in the stage of make it or break it, but I had been through too much battle to lose this one. So I reminisced of my yesteryears to see the little accomplishment that I had from the past and used it to help me today, to help myself fight the battle of drug addiction. But while on bail, I still didn't care about my problem and still hung out with the Hit Squad around the corner of Paradise, serving fiends during the day; and in the evening, Sammie and I would attend meetings, trying both AA and NA, but none of them worked for me. With every meeting that we went to, it would only be halfway through, and I would be out the door, with Sammie trailing right behind me. That girl loved me to the core, did anything for me, and in this lifetime, I don't think I'll ever experience the same love from anyone else. So special, so sweet, such a pleasure, and she never brought up the bad things or the past, always cheering me up with delight; she was a good thing, and like all the good things for me, it just didn't last. I went to prison; she died in a car crash. I know Sammie would have loved to see me one last time, before she died, maybe calling out my name as she breathed her last.

CHAPTER 69

We were coming from Steve B. Welch's parents' house that particular day. Both of them are good honest citizen, who go to church every Sunday and pray every night for their children and selves for wrongdoings that are sinful in God's eyes. I liked them; they were nice folks, never said anything. We could call them day or night; when we needed them, they'd be there. Well, we happened to have a car problem; Steve B. Welch called home, and the dad came to get the thing running for us. Sometimes, when we were so broke, they gave us a break from having to commit crime; they would help us out with $40 or $60 so that we can score. I don't know if it was good or bad that they were doing this for us, but that's love to me! Maybe they used to be drug users themselves back in their day, and they understood. This is one of those cases, as we were both broke and needed some shit. Steve B. Welch phoned his father, and he told us to come and get the cash. We only got $30, $20 from the dad and $10 from the mom. Even though they knew that I was on drugs, they still accepted me, having nothing bad to say about me, and I appreciated them a lot for it. We were cruising on McHenry, trying to get to Riverside, trying to take the back road of Miller, looking for some crystal. Coming to the four stop signs on El Vista and Riverside Rd., the police turned left to tailgate us, so I told Steve B. Welch to turn into the driveway of whom we had no clue; when he did, the cruiser just rolled by us like nothing happened, or as he was paying no attention to us, who looked close to normal and all tweaked out. But the patrol officer caught the plate, ran it, and it came back stolen, so backup was being called, and we were surrounded before we even had a chance to try and make our escape. Both of us were being taken to the MPD, and after the interview with the U.S. master postal agent about some mine that I didn't know nothing about, I was once again transferred to Stanislaus County Jail. This time, bail was set at a quarter mill. Again, I collect called to Sammie; I was out not even a whole week and had not paid off the last bail with Woody. She was fed up and had come to a conclusion that I was better off in jail than out on the streets running around. She accepted my call like always; only this time, she told me, "I'm sorry, Tommy, I love you and all, but I can't help you out this time." So I called Woody on my own, but he, too, didn't want to deal with me anymore, because I skipped bail on him. I was mad at the world now, as everyone turned me down, frustrated that I was locked up and no one could help me get out. I even tried friends outside, but they didn't provide the type of service I needed help with. I was really stuck now. As God had said, "If I imprison you, who can get you out?" And when I tried by bailing out, he put me right back in jail. While I was in jail, mother and daughter got into an argument as Sammie asked her to help with bailing me out.

"My daughter, I know that you love your Tommy, but he's not good for you, you can do better and now is a good chance for us to get away from him and his stupidity and we can start a new life somewhere else." Ruth tried to think for Sammie, as she felt it was a mother's job and meant less responsibility to do so, or maybe Ruth was trying to make Sammie see that I was nothing more than just a loser. "Look at how you are be being treated, my daughter, chasing him around, and if he has any common sense, he'll understand how much you love him, but he don't have no brain and he will never change his way or he would have done so by now. But, no, Tommy doesn't want to change, or be a father to your poor Cryxtal and Diamond," Ruth finished.

And Sammie began, "Mother, I thank you for bringing me into this world, and for giving me life, but if you ask me to choose, I want you to know, that I won't be persuaded and I'm sticking to my husband."

"My daughter, don't be too irrational with your thinking, and if you need some more time to think, I'll be here with you," Ruth tried to comfort Sammie.

"My mind is made up a long time ago, and I'm not going to turn back on myself, or lie to my heart, my love, and my desire. If you happen to think that Tommy is too much for you, then you can forget about him, me, and my children because what you are doing right now are not right, trying to break up a family, your own at that. You should be ashamed of yourself, mother. But, no matter what, I want you to know, and keep in your heart of how much I love you, but right now a part of my family is in trouble. And you only want to add burden. So if you're not in this with me, then alone, I will follow my heart and be true to myself to the end regardless of with or without your help," Sammie reassured her mother, who was dumbstruck by Sammie's words.

CHAPTER 70

"My child, your mother only speak what old age sees, and that is, he is not good for you or for my grandchildren," Ruth conceded.

"Mother, please speak only for yourself," Sammie cut her mother's sentence short, but Ruth continued.

"On second thought, you are right about your love, and since you are so firm in your belief, I, too, am with you on your choice whether you're wrong or right. I'm here for you, my daughter. We will laugh and cry together and whatever else life may bring, okay, my daughter?" Ruth's reassuring words really got Sammie happy inside, which put a smile on Sammie's face, and she hugged her mother with tears lingering in her eyes because she knew that her mother was right, but she just couldn't let Tommy go; she believed that when her loved one was in trouble and needed her the most, that was when she gotta do all that she can, but at the same token, Sammie knew that I was better off behind bars than out on the streets. She made sure I was eating good, and every visit, which she never missed, she would remind me to get a lot of rest. My store was always to the max; so were my phone card. My Cryxtal and Diamond were growing. Cryxtal was more and more like her mother, and Diamond was nothing like his sister; unlike Cryxtal, he was unclear and without a sense of my predicament. With the story that I told about my going to prison, I got my own self feeling fearful more than Sammie. I had four or five charges on my head, but for now I had my craving for the drug to fight.

After many days of eating and sleeping, Sammie told me, "You look good, baby!" during our visit, but inside, my whole body ached; every joint hurt, and eating and food intake was a pain. If you're talking about gas, I cut loose all day long.

My bunkie hated me for being his celly, because I would fart nonstop; every couple of minutes or so, I let one loose.

My canteen helped me out, as I told Ting, "Come on, man! We bunkie so we share everything, and if you hungry, my wife will look out for us. Don't worry about nothing." I told him already Sammie went online and found out about family visits; when I mentioned it to her, she told me that she had the web page already set up and ready to be downloaded and saved, with the printout of the visiting form filled out, and everything else that needed to be done. This girl was a perfectionist. She planned everything out way ahead of time. She hired me a lawyer and told her to pretend to be a public defender. I was looking at something like twelve years, because of some of the crimes committed while I was on bail, and I had three bail enhancements alone, and that was two years apiece, plus my prison prior, and my new charges. During all that time that I was sitting in jail, there was not one of my smoker friends who thought of me enough to send me a thirty-nine-cent-stamp "What's up!" letter. I was not even worth that much to them, or anyone else, besides my Sammie, whose love for me was pure and without fault, making me a God to worship and serve.

CHAPTER 71

It happened that I got transferred to the Honor Farm, and Sammie was down for me more than Bonnie for Clyde. At the farm, they had a couple of barracks and a two-story housing unit on the other side of the fence, with the basketball court to separate them from each other. Behind the farm was a river; in front was the open field. To one side was the public park, and on the east side were the rich green orchards; and under the cover of the almond trees, Sammie risked her own freedom just to sneak in a propane tank and torch, a glass pipe, lighters, crystal, and cigarettes into the farm for me. I received mail from her every day, pictures of her, and the children. Out of nowhere, as I was inside the barrack bathroom, hitting the glass pipe, my name was being called for a lawyer visit. Lawyer? It was like, what the fuck, because I was ready to plea out and take the eight-year deal; but the supposed-to-be public defender who really was a street lawyer named Delores saved me three years of freedom, and much thanks goes to my Sammie, as she was the one who came up with the money. I was ready to take the five-year deal and start my time after Delores had advised me, "If the jury find you guilty, which they will because of your prior, and physical evidence and when that happens, you're going to get the max, and it could be up to fifteen years."

On hearing fifteen, I was like, "You didn't try lower than the five years?"

"That's the lowest I can do for you."

"How about joint suspended?"

"Out of the question," she said, but she was fucking lying and only went with what Sammie had paid her to do. Delores could've gotten me less, but Sammie was already up on things, understanding how long the crystal meth stayed in the system, how long it took for the drug to be completely out of the body, and so on and so forth. This girl was a genius overnight; she had turned to take charge of the outside, my life, and situation, orchestrating everything. And at the rate she was going, she probably could get me into a prison of her choice, but it didn't happen; and for some reason, since I had been sitting in jail, she seemed to be more alive, active, and freed from her worries that had been weighing her down. This change really played tricks with my mind; even with her promise, I was still feeling insecure, because my heart had been broken before.

She reassured me that when I got out, things were going to be so much better; she said, "I have a grand plan for us, don't worry about me going out on you, or cheating on you, I'm human not no animal. So I have to respect myself as one. You're my first, and no matter what, you will be my last. I love you too much, Tommy."

"Don't change on me, because if you do, I don't think I would know how to act," I replied. Each visit seemed to be shorter and shorter as we enjoyed our time together. It was behind glass; but to Sammie it was better than chasing me around, not knowing what I was up to, when or where I was going to be smoking my dope at, and/or possibly maybe in trouble, got beat up, or arrested, overdosed, etc. It was only recently that Sammie had a full night's sleep, knowing that her big baby was saved from the dangerous drug that could claim his life at any given moment at the wrong place and time.

CHAPTER 72

I got up early on the Thursday that I was supposed to go take my plea bargain. I did some early morning push-ups before breakfast; while eating, a list of name was being called for those who had court. We were entitled to a shower before we took a ride to the downtown courthouse. I did some praying in my cell and some more on the transportation van. Coming to the underground entrance, the transportation van halted, waited for the gate to open, went around the little curves, and parked right next to the big green bin. The deputy opened the door and slammed it back close once he was out. He went through the toe-size grill door, secured his weapon inside one of the saved boxes, and came back to slide the van door open, pulling out the step ladders for the convicts to step out so that we wouldn't trip or fall, as the shackles were too short for our feet to reach the ground. Lining up against the wall, we had to face against it for safety reasons. All of us were being unloaded. The sliding door slammed back close. We were ordered to follow the guy ahead of us, going past the grill door, past a heavy-looking metal door, and entering the tunnel that lead to the lonely dungeon that awaited all of us. The steel grill door that was in the center of the tunnel was being unlocked by giant-size keys, which made a real loud clicking noise that was painful to the ears. I don't remember being this depressed before in my life, so lonely and out of place. We were told to stop and listen for our names before we could come and pass through the middle grill door, which was next to the stairway that led up to the main jail. A list was pulled out, and one by one we were being packed into a smelly shithole to wait for court; the room was empty with nothing but cold metal benches. There was the dirty toilet, and when I tried to take a piss, it was already clogged up with shit. I almost threw up at the sight; it was more gross than seeing people's head blown away. The benches and toilet were of the same worn-out black, and the walls were of beige color, but it had long lost its shine as it took on the toil of tagging, and the gang names that members want to make known to other rival gangs on the walls. There was a big writing of "Jesus loves you"; and there were carvings of arts, names, dates, and so and so was here, and so on and so forth. But the word "Jesus loves you" reminded me of Father Robert; that was what he used to tell me, and also he'd tell me about Hitler and how his greatness started from behind bars. There was something great about this hellhole, and from this dungeon, I had experienced heaven and hell while still living and didn't have to be dead or resurrected to feel the wrath of good and evil. Both hands and legs were shackled up, making every move uncomfortable and making it difficult to sit, and I couldn't even stand for long; my ass would get numb from the cold wall and metal bench. When I tried to stand up, my wrist hurt, and when I turned on my side to lie down, it burned. I tried to lie down and go to sleep; someone farted in my face. Everything about the dungeon was dark, and full of torture, not only physical pain as the wrists and ankles ached. The heart, soul, and mind were also being bothered, disrupted, without peace. The pain of isolation sometimes made my heart skip a beat and had me taking deep breaths to bring my pounding heart back to normal. This was pure hell, forever burning in the lake of agony, with sorrow of the heart and anguish of the soul without rest; for some, the dungeon is a place where all hope is gone, as they will never have a chance to return back to the outside world, which is heaven. I died once before inside this cell and personally had went to hell to experience what the lake of fire was like, and it was forever burning without relief, versus the outside, where you are free to go, do, eat, play, etc., watching little children come close and have contact with animals at the zoo, feeding seagulls and pigeons at the park, or going to the beaches in Paradise.

CHAPTER 73

The world was too huge for one man to go up against, and no one knew this better than I did. When I came to find out that Cambodia was only the size of Oklahoma State, and just with a small piece of the earth, I was lost for a decade. So imagined the whole earth. I tried to block my thoughts out, trying not to think of the outside world, and as I couldn't block them out and couldn't find the answer to my wondering mind, I moved away from the cold vent that was blowing out stinky air. Sitting on the bench after court call, it was empty, most of the inmate out. I tried not to let my back touch the wall, because of the spit and mucus that had been building up over the years. I didn't have to try and eavesdrop on the conversation that the elder Caucasian man with a tall nose, deep-set eyes, gray hair, and a mustache was having. He was telling his young companion who had a drug problem, and for a young man, the youngster did look shot out—rotten teeth when he smiled, hair all stringy, with sinking eyes like how mine used to be, cheekbones hella exposed, hella sucked up like he was only made out of bone and skin with no muscle nor meat nor any fat. The elder man was telling the youngster about a seven to nine months drug program they have down South called Norco or NRCC, where even if your sentences is five or six years, if you are accepted in the program and you complete it, you have a chance to clear your record. I liked what I was hearing, but my record was already beyond repair; but my desire was to be free, and if I can cheat and escape my prison sentences, that was what I wanted to do. I had second thoughts about going to prison; besides, I did have a drug-abuse problem and needed serious help. The conversation was cut short when the sheet metal door slid open. Keys rattling, a CO came to a halt in front of the grill door and unlocked it in the same fashion as the last deputy. He jiggled the key back into his key chain on his wrist and pulled out a list from his pocket down by the kneecap. All the names on the list were highlighted. Names were called. Allen Johnson, Johnny Smith,

Tony Montana, Tha Thing, Taylor, Soto, Damn-Long Sothin, and so on, till the whole dungeon cleared out, except for the gray-haired white man. We stole a glance at each other. I turned to look at the two thugs in the far corner, away from the odor of the shit sitting in the toilet, and across was the OG homie I, in a yellow jumpsuit, fighting a three strikes case. He was pacing the floor as to escape his misery ahead or the punishment that awaited him, as he didn't know what lay ahead of him, or to block out the hurt by the people from the outs. I was thinking about my own pain and had to take a deep sigh. I was disrupted when the gray-haired man busted out, "What you're in here for?"

I looked around to make sure he was talking to me before I answered, "Well, I have a couple of charges," and I handed him my papers, which had all my charges. He studied the papers, then he handed them back to me, and in my mind, I told myself, *Another jailhouse lawyer.*

"What's the deal?" he asked.

"Five years."

"Five years! Man, this guy has doubled your charges and he got three years," he said. I heard enough, but he wouldn't stop. "You got a lawyer?"

"No! I only have a public defender."

"What's the name?" he went on.

"Delores."

"Delores," he repeated and brushed his beard, before he said, "I never heard of her before. Is she young?" I was like, *Shut the fuck up already*, but he didn't. "You from the Modesto Hit Squad?

"Yeah! That's what I bang, Hit Squad, why?" I asked, at the same time getting ready to defend my gang; but it turned out, I was talking to a J-cat, who didn't mean any harm and just wanted to converse, have someone to talk to.

CHAPTER 74

The people that went to court had almost all came back, and half of them were already back at their assigned housing; still my name had not been called, and when they finally did call, I had a chance to talk to Delores. She gave me instruction to say, "Yes! Yes! Yes!" to everything the judge said or asked. Since my case was closed before the court started with the plea bargain, I was the last one out of courtroom number 7. Sammie managed to blow me a kiss and did a phone sign with her thumb and pinky and brought it to her ear and mouth to tell me to call her. I did, because I once again felt I was at the lowest point of my life. When I got sentenced, I got transferred back to the PCS to await my trip to Tracy State Prison, the reception center for the surrounding county and Central Valley. Before, the gray goose used to come pick inmates up from the county. Now, the county transferred inmates to the states. I was awakened out of my sleep by the graveyard officer and was told, "Pack all your belongings, and paperwork," and it was two in the morning. At 4:00 AM, the door popped open by the controller up front; from here the waiting started. We waited in the dayroom for another two hours till 6:00 AM; from here we got chained up and led out of the unit to the waiting tank for another two hours. 8:00 AM, the transportation officer arrived with a suitcase full of files and another full of cuffs and shackles. One by one our names were being called to the front controller desk, to double-check, to make sure they were taking the right inmates to the right place. "Tommy Ok." And on hearing my last name, one of the officers that overheard it repeated, "Tommy OK! Is that how you say your last name, OK?" The clowning officer turned to ask. I could be a smart mouth and make him look stupid by showing him Oklahoma's abbreviation, OK. But this is not the time for fun and games; besides, these CO will find ways to hurt you and get away with it. They are not to be played with. Yes! Sometimes people do call me Tommy OK, and I'm okay with both, but Ok is my last name.

"You can't take the book and the magazine, it's the county's property," the short CO lady announced as she took everything out of the box that I packed my stuff in. We have to go through the metal detector and out to the open air. December was awfully cold in the morning, and with the chilly wind, it didn't help. The chain that wrapped around my wrists and ankles felt like ice. Even though it had been a while since I got myself in trouble, the uncomfortable feeling and the pain of losing my freedom took me back to the time when I was confined in the little monkey cage back in my country, when I was caught trying to escape from the hand of the Khmer Rouge. It was too painful for me to reminisce, so I quickly shook the memory out of my head, and with my past experience, I found a source to help me get through that hard time, which was much easier compared to the cage.

CHAPTER 75

My left arm went numb, where the cuff sat on my wrist. The mark on it carved in my skin, touching the bone, making me feel, not only the pain, but lost and out of place in a stage of confusion without relief to my heart and everything in a disarray of thoughts, feelings, emotions, which were disturbing. "Can it get any worse?" I asked myself, going through the R and R (receiving and release). We were told to take everything off once the cuffs were removed and before we went through the grill door. Inside, there was a line of four or five correctional officers inspecting our everything—mouth, tongue out and up, moving fingers around your gum and ears, running a hand through your hair, hands out, turn, up, your nuts, sucking your dick, turn around, feet, left side, right side, bend down at the knees and give three honest coughs. Going through the metal detector, inmate workers threw you an orange jumpsuit, while the other asked for your shoes size (Jap flaps) during orientation. On the wall was a picture of John Wayne, and the CO that was conducting the orientation asked the new arrivals, "Do you know who that is?" pointing to John Wayne's photo.

I have learned this type of shit early on, about these types of games that were designed by the CO to clown inmates, and sure enough, one dumbass barked out, "John Wayne."

The power-tripping elder Mexican CO said, "That's right, and on the other side of this fence, there's a lot of them. So you might not know what you will run into, so my advice to you is best to stay to yourself, do your time and go home, and don't be the Chucky Cheese with his tail wrapped around his legs. You can make your time hard for yourself, or you can do your time easy, and get out.

"Now, remember," he said, pacing the outer side of the fence, "you are going to run into a lot of problem, but don't worry or be scared, just come running to one of us, and we'll take care of you." He was all smiling now, as he was proud of his job, looking at dicks hanging all day. I didn't know how tired you can get from just being cold and staying in one place; I didn't have to wrestle long once I was assigned to a cell. After I made my bed, got under the grayish issued blanket with everything still on, I was out for the count. I woke up to another day of life in America behind bars, waiting in line for chow; looking around me, I see a bunch of dead men walking, including myself. Going to and from, I questioned myself, *Is this the city of refuge, or is it the time and place that is set for everyone, including myself, to be at?* I was taught and learned that the body was there, but the spirit was trapped; and the soul couldn't go nowhere, and a lot of us like myself were going through the same pain and suffering without escape. If it was not this, it was that; but everybody's life is in miseries, and full of it—the agony of heartache, hatred, betrayal, anxiety, excitement, thrill, and everything else. As we couldn't wait to get out, our desire increased in wanting to do things, and most important of all was to fuck. Pussy was on every convict's mind, including mine; none of us could wait to fuck any female's brains out.

CHAPTER 76

Sammie, Cryxtal, and Diamond came to see me first thing when visiting hours started. And since I had not been housed, the visits had to be between glass, always for the fuckin' safety purpose. For the first time in my life, I started to see something as I watched my children played, and I realized that I was a father. And when I talked to Sammie about different subjects, of all the trolls and the dead men walking, she told me, "Tommy, you're older than I am and been through a lot, been in and out of predicaments. You've done and dealt with different situations. You have turned predicaments of no hope around and got something out of the hard experiences before. Now if you ask me"—she paused then continued—"I say if your mind can bring you to see all these dead men walking, then you can bring yourself to see the opposite because there are always two sides of things with everything in life." For once I paid close attention to Sammie's words, and what she said made a lot of sense. I thought about it a little more.

Waking up one Sunday morning, my Christian bunkie told me, "Today is special. We're having grand slam for breakfast." I acted like I didn't know what he was talking about; just because a new number was given to me, he assumed I was a new booty. I wasn't worried about the breakfast, but if I missed it, I have to miss getting a lunch sack; and if some shit might jump off, the institution might go on a lockdown, the kitchen will be closed down, and dinner won't be til 10-12:00 at night in the cell. And when they were finished serving what had been cooked, everybody else will get a sack lunch for breakfast; and I had come to hate the taste of the foul-smelling turkey meat for lunch, dinner, and breakfast. I couldn't wait to go to the store and stock up on top Roman soup. And on store day (canteen), when I went, I bought Sammie a Valentines card; and this was the first present I ever bought her that had any meaning, and it was the last. On a Monday, I had a ducat to go to the medical office at 8:00 AM, but they pulled me out at 4:00 AM, unpopped the door, and we exited the building with an inmate worker handing me my lunch sack for breakfast. In the clinic, they asked of my medical condition and the medication being taken if any, and so on and so forth, only to be told by the nurse to go back outside in the freezing cold, shrivel up my nut sack, and wait for my name to be called so I can get my blood drawn.

"After this, you can go back to your cell." And forty-eight hours later, a nurse came around the cell, checking the BT shot. I felt sorry for the taxpayers as I saw how easy these state workers made their money. I even envied them, but mostly I felt sorry for myself, because all my life I had been without a family or friends and was now stuck in a cell. I only knew the word "easy," but I never experienced it or had life easy. Going to dinner at the main kitchen, we went past the church that I had never took notice before; looking inside, I saw Father Robert. It had been a long while since I last picked up the Bible, to the point that I was afraid to touch the Holy Book. Here at DVI (Dual Vocational Institute), reading materials were hard to come by. So you were stuck in a two-man cell without nothing to read, and after a while push-ups didn't even help pass the time. In my case, I was alone; my Christian celly got transferred to Folsom, and out of boredom, I reached out for the Bible. And as my hand touched it, I felt a chill all over my body, remembering what Father Robert had told me, how I needed to read the Bible over and over, again and again every day. The predicament that I was in right then had come to the moment, the moment to reconnect with a higher power. It was the perfect time and the right place for my spiritual life to begin. I realized that this was my chance to start over again. Everything was beginning to change, starting with my thoughts. I decided what I was doing and thinking would be the opposite of the doings and actions that I had taken before that time, letting go of my sick mind, my destructive way of life—such as smoking dope and crystal, playing dice, betting, and gambling. Instead of sitting at the table slapping cards like everybody else on the yard, I made up my mind to dedicate myself to learning, picking up where I left off when I walked out of Father Robert's house. I started to see things with different eyes and came to believe that "prison is the best school that money can't buy." I started to see all these walking, dead men as professionals in some fields, and who could get a better training than from the experience itself?

CHAPTER 77

Back to Sara Long, she had caught wind of my incarceration; while I was locked up, life for her went from bad to worse as she picked up a gambling habit because of self-disappointment and for losing a good thing and being brokenhearted. If it weren't for her children, she had no reason to live. So she lived and was going with the motion of waking up every day, going to work like everybody else, and supporting the family. From past experiences, she knew that when I was locked up, I didn't have no one. So to redeem herself, she saw a perfect opportunity for her to act and reach out with sincerity to make amends. She did a little research and found out the prison I was housed at. On April 30, a Cambodian New Year weekend, I was happy and looking forward to see my wife and kids, expecting a visit. I got ready again. My name was being called for the visit. I was excited as I tried to look my best for my family. I dressed up in a stately blue outfit, was clean shaved, hair slicked back, and was going at almost a run to the visit room. But when I walked into the visiting room, I spotted the wrong family that I had in mind. On entering the visiting room that Saturday the thirtieth, on seeing Sara and her family in place of Sammie, Cryxtal, and Diamond, it took all my thrill away, and the cloud of sorrow took over when she told me what happened to Ruth and Sammie. Tears rained down my cheeks.

Back in Lawton, Mr. Cooper was growing impatient by the day as he didn't hear from me, and he decided to get some peace of mind by asking Sue Upchurch to come search for me. When she was inquired by Mr. Copper about coming to look for me, she gladly took the offer, as she had also been missing me and been wanting to see me. So this was perfect for her, and she wasted no time in starting out in her Ford van; coming with flat tire and all, Sue Upchurch made it to Modesto, but with the same problems that Sammie had. Sue, too, didn't know my a.k.a. was Flea; on finding out, she laughed at "Flea," and on second thought, she thought that it fitted me. Flea was home from one end of the earth to the other side of the world, and now he found himself locked up. Sue made up her mind to stick around, wait for me to get out, telling herself "good things come to those who wait," and she intended to take me back to Lawton where I belonged, with her.

CHAPTER 78

From Tracy DVI, I was transferred to Soledad State Prison. They housed me on the central yard, and as things were chaotic for me on the outside, so was the inside; as the Viet and Samoan went at it because of misunderstanding, all the "others" went on lockdown. Since it was the Asian and the Pacific Islander, we stayed locked down the longest, fucking up visit and store, missing out on the action and everything else in the yard. No phone call, no hustling, no nothing. So when my first visit came around after getting out of lockdown, I was excited. Going into the visiting room with my head up and chest out, as Sue Upchurch had taught me how to carry myself, I was looking for Sammie, Cryxtal, and Diamond; but instead I saw Sara Long, Elisabeth, Alexandria, and baby Johnathan. I was confused and was like, "What the fuck!" as I was making my way toward them; two things came to my mind. One, she was not on my visiting list, and second, who was she visiting? My thoughts turned to Sammie and hoped she doesn't blame me for Sara and her family being there and get mad at me.

My daughter, Elisabeth, burst out, "Hello, Daddy! You look good, Father," taking all the words out of my mouth from what I wanted to say.

After brief hugs and kisses, Sara wasted no time and got to the point. "When are you coming home?" The question alone was puzzling, so I stayed put and quiet and looked around for my loved ones. "I miss you, Athom." The way she made it sound, there was a sincere ring in her voice, but when we locked eyes, she reminded me, "I'm here only for the kids." That was what her mouth said, but inside, her emotion ran wild; she had other things on her mind that she held back from letting out, like the fact that she still loved me and missed me very much and couldn't wait till I get out so she could take me home and fuck my

---

158

brains out with no grease in her asshole. You know, I started the conversation, breaking the silence, with all kinds of noises around us.

"First and foremost, I want to thank you for your time, and I greatly appreciate the visit. It's very thoughtful of you to bring my children for me to see, and I want you to understand that what we had and went wrong in the past are gone." I continued, "Yesterday is nothing more than a good or bad memory. Everything is gone, and had passed away. The present time is ours, especially right now, this very moment that we call today. The present is a vision of the future, our best day to live is today. Many days, many weeks, many months, and many years has fly by, and some moments we cherished, and others we learned from. Some lessons are good for us and have strong effects on others. In ways that they can benefit others of no good or gain to anyone not even self. In my mind I kept all the memories and that's where my past stays. But no matter what, yesterday's gone. Gone is time, and it don't wait for no one, or stop to give you another chance to go back. Now let us not take today for granted. Enjoy this little time together, and try to make it a fun moment for everyone." I thanked her.

CHAPTER 79

"Please, Sara, don't call me Athom because I hated that life of mine. Besides, it's dead and buried back in Cambodia," I explained to her. "I know I haven't been a perfect angel and I have made more mistakes than most. That's because from birth, I was cursed. I have no guidance with all the odds stacked against me. So if you think that I have wronged you, or harmed you in any kind of way, from the bottom of my heart, I ask that you believe me. I've never meant anything bad for you. It's just that things are not working out and I have to admit that it's my fault." I stopped to look at her, who had given the bottle to young Johnathan; on her silence, I continued taking my time to study Alexandria more closely and saw young Chantho—just how I remembered her. I looked over to see if Sara was done before I went on, "Now for whatever reason you are here, I want to make any misunderstanding on my part between us clear, and I want you to forgive me for all my mistakes and my wrongs that are in your eyes. I know I only got myself to blame for what happened between us, and by the way, why are you here anyway? And how did you get on my visiting list anyhow?" With this question, I only got Sara looking at me all stupid, like it was something I should have already known. "Oh well," I said.

And she told me, "I'm already on your visiting list long before that bitch Sammie of yours was even around. Besides, I'm not here for you. I'm here for the kids and to bring you this newspaper clipping."

But I was interrupted by Alexandria. "Daddy?"

"Yes, my dear baby?" I sweetly replied.

"You like my new hair, and my new look?"

"Beautiful, just like your mother." Sara was secretly flattered and smiled to herself.

"I'm going to start school, Daddy," she went on. "Preschool—"

Then Elisabeth burst the bubble, "Daddy! You know what?"

"What, Daughter?"

"Mommy still loves you."

"I love her too. But, that's as far as I got. But nothing—"

Sara cut me short and concluded, "I bring the kids here to visit you, and not to talk about my personal life, or love." Sara was heated.

"I apologize for being such a child," I told her.

"Yeah! That's all you are is a kid trapped inside a man's body and need to grow up. You're twenty-five, but you think like five. That's why I can't stand you."

"Oh! Now I know why you leave me behind at mango city, back in Cambodia, when I needed you most because I was too much of a child for you, and you needed a father figure." I brought up the past, because I couldn't believe that that was how she thought of me. With the statement, Sara went silent, which left me confused, so I turned my attention to the newspaper that she brought; on setting my eyes on the headline and discovering that it was the news of the death of my beloved Sammie, my heart damn-near stopped. I couldn't breath, and my soul drowned in sadness. This was the hardest time of my life.

CHAPTER 80

Upon peeping the almost rolled-up newspaper clipping of the *Modesto Bee* front page, my eyes caught the big bold black letters across the paper. It read, CAR ACCIDENT. "Two dead, no survivors," was the subheading. In the middle was the picture of the crash vehicle that I knew too well. A brownish colored MVP's front end was halfway smashed in, one wheel gone, windshield looked to have a hole in it, and a door was opened on the driver side; under the photo, in red, it read, "Mother and daughter going out, and had a little too much fun, and one glass of alcohol too many. The driver was dead on arrival, and passenger Sammie Ok flew out through the front windshield, and was dead before she even hit the ground. She went about fifty feet into the air on impact." This was all I could take; I couldn't read on, and my mind quickly turned to my Cryxtal and Diamond, and worry took over. I wondered where they were right then, and if they were okay and well. I almost had a heart attack and had to take hold of my chest. Sara tried to relax me. "Calm down. It's okay. I have the children with me, and they are with my grandparents right now, while I came to let you know what had happened to your wife and mother-in-law." When she said this, there was something evil in her eyes, and she had the smile of Lucifer's daughter-in-law. I couldn't stand her sinister face or continue the visit. My mind was on what had happened to my wife; my Cryxtal's and Diamond's well-beings were my concern. I wondered if Map knew about the tragic accident.

"I really am sorry, but can we cut our visit kinda short, because my head is elsewhere," I pleaded with Sara; I was deaf to all the noise around me. I explained to Sara that it was nothing personal; it was just that I wanted to give 'em my full attention.

And her response was, "I'm only here for the kids and to bring you the good news of the fucking dead bitch of yours." On hearing this, I wanted to just choke the daylight out of her, but as a father, I knew it was not appropriate for my children to see their adult parents argue and fight, plus that would only lead me to the hole. So I bit all my words and turned to all my children, even though my mind was thinking of my dead loved one. Sadness had taken over, and I was drowning in my own sorrow. I was going down in pain, and my heart was anchored to hurt; my soul couldn't go nowhere, trapped as I was physically behind the prison wall. Everything inside of me wanted to come out—the cries, the tears, the fear, the sadness, the anguish, the agony, but mostly my freedom. I was locked up and couldn't even attend my, rest in peace, wife's funeral to bid 'em my last good-bye!

When I got back to my cell, my celly, a Hmong homie Vang Yeng, who always looked forward to hear the good and exciting news about my visits as always, asked the same question after all my visits, "So, how was it?" He wanted to know, but I was in so much of everything to respond, so I just handed him the front page clipping that I had ripped out into smaller and smaller pieces so I can have it sneaked in through the inmate workers. Taping it to the bottom of the mop bucket and getting past the CO, it cost me a can of good smoking Bugler, but it was worth it; even if it cost more, I would have paid for the news. While Vang was reading the paper, I jumped up to my top bunk, got under the blanket, turned to the wall on my side, and I cried and cried and cried. I didn't go to chow or the yard or did any of the things that I normally did. But how can I? I was in too much sorrow and deep misery, and my biggest worry was about Cryxtal and Diamond; they worried me sick, forcing me into meditation and into what I was secretly going through, feeling the pain that nobody knew but me and my body. I hid my deepest fears, scares, tears, cries, and the thoughts of me wanting to die with my Sammie, inside.

Chapter 81

Where was the jubilation, and when would the celebration come, and had the end of my misery came? Then in one of my deepest meditations that lasted over half a day, I saw the pain that I was in. I was hurt to the point of death and saw life as nothing more than just a box of chocolates full of surprises; my whole life was filled with surprises of aches and pains. From birth, the cycle had not changed, and where there was happiness, I only received hurt and shame; when I found love, came the motherfucking game to be followed by the burning pain. I wished it would end, but it went round and round, again and again, too many years of tears without relief and full of damn shame. Sorrow had been my best friend, and sadness never let me go. Dejection, depression, grief, and oppression was close to my heart. My soul had been under heavy pressure, and my brain was without ease. Pain had been with me since birth, and it was going to be a part of me till my dying day. I tried everything, even praying, but my pain just didn't go away, and my sorrow didn't stop. The longer I saw daylight, the longer, deeper, and harder I felt desolated in my own world of being lost, hopeless, and having misfortunes, leaving me with the same question that I didn't have the answer for: "Why me? Is there really an oasis in the dry dessert?"

"Fuck that shit," I said, as I was coming out of my soul-searching. I told myself, "It's time, time is all I have with me, now that I'm not a part of Sammie and her world, but her words are still alive and active."

"Tommy! Sometimes, you have to come to yourself, and start doing things the opposite because that's the start to all changes. If you want the fire to stop burning, then don't add wood," were her exact words. This was all I had of my wife to ponder on; and while I went into my own world thinking, I was blessed to have my good friend Vang, who understood. When my money ran dry, and I couldn't make it to the canteen, he fed me every night and made sure I went to sleep with a full stomach, without complaint—that's a real friend. Am I grateful for him, and for Sara Long, as she brought all of my children once in a while to visit me on weekends, making me think once again differently of her; and her staying in touch was only making me fall in love with her all over again, and I let it be known to her shortly after, as I don't know how to hold nothing back because I'm a man who speaks his mind.

CHAPTER 82

My dearest Chantho, you are the one, my true love from the beginning. God, you and I already know, I love you above all else, more than my own life. You mean so much to my spirit and my soul; you're the one who saves me, preserves me, and gives me life to live this long, even though you left me alone. But at the same time, every time I'm wrong, you come through. Even though you have made my life a living hell, your wonderful love is also unconditional. I love you, Chantho, more than I dare to let you know with my every fiber how much you mean to me. Well, as you know, I'm not much on letter writing, because I started school at fifth grade and dropped out at tenth grade, but I'm working on my education, so I'mma leave you room to think of me. Chantho, you are more right, more noble, and more beautiful to me right now more than ever before. As precious as you are to me, together we're gonna raise a family. I love you, Chantho, always have, and forever will be staying true; remember how you have loved me from the start and please never, ever let me go again, because we belong together to no end. We are soul mates from heaven, so let us not break something that God had joined together. I miss you more than words can say; I can't wait to come home and make sweet love to you all day. Smile for me; I'll see you on the weekend. Good night, sweetheart, and don't forget to give all the children a kiss for me. Love you always, and all I'm asking is that you would try to love me the same way too.

Tommy Ok

P.S. Please send photos of everybody. Thank you!

This was one of the hardest letters to write; besides, English is my second language, second like everything else in life, because my will inside that fires up my desire to crave and want and not give up, that's what makes me the number one.

CHAPTER 83

The visit came without delay from Sara and the children, and the siblings were growing along with each passing week. Alexandria wanted me to come home. "Daddy! Can you come home with us?"

My heart was broken with her desire; I forced myself to tell her, "Not yet, my daughter."

"Soon, Daddy?" she wanted to know.

"Yeah! Soon, my daughter, okay?" She accepted the "soon" for an answer and went back to playing with her siblings. They seemed to be getting along better than I anticipated. I thought that my Cryxtal and Diamond would get slapped around, but that didn't seem to be the case; it turned out that Sara was a better mother than I thought, and knowing that I was happy, Sara told me that the custody paper she filed had went through. A relief, I sat back and studied Sara, sitting in her plastic chair, and wondered if she knew how I felt; she seemed to feel proud of herself for redeeming herself. *Now I have to make him see that I'm the best thing for him*, Sara kept in mind.

"Daddy! I have to go to the dentist to get my teeth fixed. Look, Daddy, I have seven silver teeth now."

And before I can respond to Alexandria, Elisabeth spoke up out of boredom and asked, "Why do we have so many grandparents, Daddy?"

I told her, "You have to ask your mother that question, my daughter." With that, she turned back to what she was doing. With this opportunity, I took my time to thank Sara. "Thank you, Sara." I had to call her by her new name because she thinks that Chantho is too Cambodian for her, and she was an American now. I thought the bitch was hella dumb for not remembering where she was from, but I went along with her stupid ass because I had my Cryxtal and Diamond to worry about, and her sorry ass was my only hope. I told her, "I'm counting on you, and you didn't let me down. My time is that much easier for me to serve. You really make my sentence lighter to bear with your help. I know talk is cheap." I continued, "But if you were in my shoes, you, too, would only have words and can only ask. Because there's nothing you can do, when you're in confinement."

She seemed to understand and replied, "Don't worry about anything. I got everything under control. All you need to do is stay out of trouble, and go to school." And went to school I did; I started out with what I needed to get into vocational, and that was to get my GED. My tab test scores were high, but at the same time, I didn't have a GED or a high school diploma to be able to get into vocational. So I signed up for the GED testing.

CHAPTER 84

Every day I worked hard on my studies and physical health, forcing myself to forget the past and start thinking of my future. Taking myself back to the day that I could remember, I wanted to clearly see where I came from, how and what helped me get here, and what I must do to get to where I was destined to be; I thought of the number of years from now, of work, energy, and time it'll take to get accomplished, and so on and so forth, to get to where I wanted to be and have what my host may desire to possess. On pondering, my own words came back to haunt me about what I told my friend, of my statement that "the time I sit in jail, will be the time that I will make the most money of my life." At the time when I told my family and friends these words, I, myself, didn't really know what I was talking about; maybe it was the tweek talk, but tweeked or not, one thing was for sure—I have to be true to myself, so I have no choice in this matter but to come up with a solution. I argued long and hard with myself, frustrated at times, and mad at myself other times. "Damn, why the fuck did I have to go around and talk about something I have no clue of how to go about doing it." But I couldn't and wouldn't give up, as I never did before on myself and on life; and like always, hard thinking made you hungry, always driving you to find a way to care. I first started out by blocking the outside world. I came to realize that no matter how much I worry about what was going on at home, there was nothing I can do to help, to make anything better or different for anyone. I told myself that I had to start from where I was at. Beginning with my self, that was actually how I never abandoned the beliefs and philosophies that I lived by. "What you see and what you hear are not the same as what you would know. Just because you heard something, it doesn't necessarily mean it's true. Start the same with what you see with my changes, and I'll bet it's not the same as you know it." For many days and restless nights, my mind fought for answers; concentrating hard all the while, the only thing that came to my mind and wouldn't go away was the fact that I wanted to be a millionaire. This much I was sure of—I wanted to be rich. The problem now was how I was going to go about becoming wealthy. As I thought about it, I saw myself slaving for a corporation nine to five; I am not geared cut to it. Even if I worked the high end and get something like $50,000 a year, it still might take me twenty years to make a million dollars after my calculation, and that was if I didn't spend a penny out of every paycheck. I threw the unsatisfactory results of working for someone else in the trash, making room for my brain cells, and moved on to something else, but it was more complicated than I want to get myself into. "Yeah, start my own business!" I said. Or real estate might even be better. But that, too, called for money; and credit was another situation, a new set of problems on its own, as I never established myself. So I went to the library and did some research to get deeper into the knowledge about credits; I did a very intent research. And I liked what I was learning, and I told myself, "Okay, real estate can come into play after the first stage, which is capital establishment." For now I had to figure out a way of how to come up with some type of income flow, one that'll be on a regular basis like clockwork, but nothing yet, as nothing concrete for me to consider doing for assets came to my mind. So I kept on studying, doing my homework til I finally came up with a solution.

CHAPTER 85

Many days went by, and many books had been read and a lot of notes were taken, but still nothing as of yet clicked in my head that would meet the kind of money I needed to make, to fit into my time frame. Every field of education I looked into required money. By now, my mind was sore, and my eyes hurt like the time when I used to go for months without sleep, tweeking my brain out. My coffee supply was running low, and cigarettes were expensive since the state removed tobacco from all the institutions—a dollar for a pinner rolled out of shit paper wrapper. Facing too many questions at one time, I had to find out what I must do at this present time. I understood that education can take you a long way. So I decided to dedicate myself to school every day, rain or shine, wet or dry, to go to class to learn and study on my off days. I would be the first one in line waiting to go to the library. Working on my practice GED test, asking anyone that can help, a month later I passed the actual test, with one point above the required score. I got my GED and quickly got on the vocational waiting list for landscaping. Three months later, I was in and was assigned to my own garden area where I got hands-on training and grading outside of class work; inside the classroom, I practiced on designing landscapes, working the legion, because this was something that I considered as something I might need to fall back on, and I also worked hard on rehabilitating myself. I started out with inspiring reading materials. I told myself, I needed to be lifted up a little. It was time to forget the past and make amends with myself. If I hoped to do anything for myself, and my children, my spirit needed to be lifted up, and to be sure that I had not gone crazy, I signed up to see a psych. I went to the clinic with my ducats, and once I was called in, I told the fat lady with short white hair that matched her outfit, I said, "I think I need some type of medication," after she told me to take a seat.

"What makes you request for psych medication, and what for?" she asked.

"I think I'm going crazy, and need some type of pills to help assist my mental health."

"Well, let me be frank with you, young man," the fat lady said. "I heard all kinds of good reasons to prescribe inmates drugs, and by far yours is the lamest I've ever heard. From my professional experience," she said, "I never knew of a crazy person to know for himself that he's crazy, or needs medication, so if you ask me, I believe that you're perfectly fine, your heartbeat sounds good, and you look like you're in a good health. All you need to do is take care of yourself, sleep good, and exercise regularly." I thanked the ugly but real nice doctor, coming out of the clinic with a smile; this was the lift up that I needed, to take myself to another level, as my potentials were being discovered and my abilities were being searched out, doing everything the opposite of the old me. And, not overnight, but overtime, my thinking and reasoning of why I do this and that and seeing things as that way and this way were beginning to change, and it was for the better.

CHAPTER 86

Every day for three and a half years, I buried myself in learning, because I wanted to be a changed man when I got out of prison this time, and I was accomplishing a whole new person, a born-again individual, not only to be a better father to my children but also to be a better person in the community as a whole. For my own personal self-help, I picked different self-help classes and programs that the institution had to offer. I took advantage of everything, achieving and accomplishing everything I put my mind into doing. Completing the bridging program that was created by the CDC, designed to help you better communicate and interact with people, it didn't take long for me to receive another certification. I also completed anger management and breaking barriers, then started on the Criminals and Gang Members Anonymous. It was a topical study workshop for (1) what we have come to realize, (2) fitting in, (3) misinterpretation of pride (self-deception to self-destruction), (4) people pleasing, (5) the arrogance within us, (6) mixed messages, (7) crime is an impulsive action, (8) the criminal lifestyle ingrained in us, (9) shortcomings will always come, (10) we argued for limitations, (11) the many forms of denial, (12) once living passion to be a criminal or gang member, and (13) now living with passion to recover from one's self. There were the Narcotics Anonymous and Alcoholics Anonymous, the twelve steps and all, and creative conflict resolutions. There was the reentry program, and I had my landscaping certification, along with my GED—all for my children, along with my desire to be a better father to them. I participated in a parenting education program, and for Father Robert, I got baptized inside the prison and successfully completed the great truth of the Bible. Most important of all, I still got my health. I started my recovery with just eating good, resting well, and walking. At the beginning, I started with a half mile for the first four weeks, and I moved up to one mile three times a week—Monday, Wednesday, and Friday. I did five sets of ten reps of push-ups and five pull-ups along with ten dips every day! I reminded myself to do the exercise and stay healthy for my children—night and day, weekend or holiday, 24-7. Every chance I get, I buried myself inside books; I even started to write poems, which I hope to have it published one day. I saw a vision of readers benefiting from my poems of my personal experiences, of my love life, liberty, and confinement, and I had to smile at my own fantasy. But the unseen is not a joke because that's where everything starts, and ideas born for everything come from the unseen rather than the seen.

CHAPTER 87

It was raining outside, and I was on my bunk reading my father's tales; but the day seemed so depressing that it got me feeling all gloomy, making me unable to concentrate on what I was reading that I had to set my entertainment of Tommy Ok's adventures down and pick up Donald Trump, but I had to set him down too. As my mind drifted to the FHRSS account that my mind had created during my study of marketing (future, home, retirement, savings, and spending), I daydreamed and wished I had the money to start stacking these imaginary accounts; I wanna be rich, and my brain didn't let me down, as something triggered my brain cells. Picking Donald back up, I turned the book around and studied it closer; turning it over in my mind, I turned to the book that I once read by Alice Potter. She wrote about nothing more than how she went about doing her regular routine, how she exercised, and how she walked her dog. I am proud to say that she is a very special friend of mine, whom I came to know through her visiting me with ink and paper, through her letters about feeding the neighbor's cat and people reading to her, admiring his work. A. Potter, as busy as she was, she made time to reach out to me; when even my bosom closet had forgotten me, she gave me the encouragement that I needed to keep going and to continue with my writing career till today. Plus with what I had picked up along the way in my art and correction classes, where I attended to learn how to write books, one of the authors clearly stated, "People will read what you write," which gave me an idea about writing books. I had read a lot of books, but I had never written a book before. So I got into a book-writing research, and after six months of stupidity study, I finished up with writing to the bone. But I didn't begin anew with creative writing, and I didn't just write anything as the book taught, because I wanted to start writing a good story, the best story, with unique tales, and an out-of-this-world kind of entertainment, something that others can learn from; and if only one person in life can be touched and be affected for the better by my trials and tribulations that I was sharing, then I knew that my time and energy had been well spent. If not, at least it was something that I could use as a tool to try and put some money in my imaginary account and turn it to reality. To be an established author was my destiny, and now it was up to me to make it come true.

CHAPTER 88

My first book took me seven months to complete, and it was the *I* story. My best work wasn't yet crafted, but I guarantee and stand by my work that it was *good*, and I didn't care about opinions because that was what caused a lot of entrepreneurs to fail, and I saw and knew this. So I chose to be real with only myself, doing my own things; with everything that I do, I make sure it's to my taste, likeness, and satisfaction. Taking care of my interests and minding my business as the Holy Bible had taught me, I dedicated myself to live for me; with this knowledge, I was inspired, and everything I did and got into only made me that much better. I had my second book done, followed by the third. But when I first started writing, everybody was in doubt about my skill and ability, including my education, but I didn't take what the next man couldn't do and made it my personal business. My focus was on my goals, and my priorities were planned out; all I had to do now was the work. Oh, I almost forgot, except for my friend Vang Yeng. He encouraged me to write every night, and when he knew that I was putting overtime into my book, he would come through with leftover dinner or Top Ramen (always beef). For me it was sad when it was time for me to go. I had to leave him behind because his release time hadn't come, but only for a short time we parted ways because he's my friend; I will never forget him. Time had come for us to part worlds, and we must had more yards than OJ, pacing the track for hours on end. Sometimes from yard open till yard close, we talked about everything, sharing opinions, working out together. We talked about other things, but it's none of your business. I got my ducats; I was going on S time, with my dress out waiting for me at the RR. Finally my time had come. Then it happened. My name was being heard over the yard's megaphone to report to the councilor's office. "Tommy Ok 77, report to the councilor's office."

I was like, "What the fuck!"

I made my way over, reported to the inmate clerk, and once I took my seat in front of my councilor, she told me, "Bad news, Tommy. Mr. Ok, you have a warrant from Stanislaus County."

I was like, "What the fuck." My councilor told me what my charge was, possession of sale, and made me sign a couple of papers and booted me out the door. I had to buy somebody's phone time to alarm Sara, for her not to come pick me up, but I couldn't reach her, so when she did come to pick me up, she only got a disappointed and sad feeling. When I phoned her after she got back home, she was sad because she was really looking forward to fucking; since she didn't get to nut, she let no one comfort her. With the short fifteen-minute phone call that I had, I tried to cheer her up as much as possible, but it was only hopeless; Sara only cried and hung up without words.

CHAPTER 89

On the morning that I was supposed to be released, the CDC dressed me out in my street clothes, but instead of going home, I was shackled up and got tossed into the gray goose going down south to LA County Jail to await my transfer back up to Modesto. LA County Jail was the worst place I had ever been before in my life on earth. When we got there, it was already dark; the bus pulled into the underground R and R parking lot. From the outside, it didn't look all that big, but inside it was hella huge. We were unloaded and went up the steps that lead into the jail. And before my cuffs and shackles were properly off, I was sized up for a fight. I was from up North and knew little about what went on down South. Little did I know, all the Khmer had the green light on 'em. "Watch your back, homies!" said the Mexican guy whose English was like mine. I wouldn't doubt he was not born here like I was not born here, and I knew what it meant by his look—trouble! I could smell it, but inside, I wished things didn't have to be this way because he was a foreigner, just as I was one, and stuck in the same predicament as I was in. And we didn't need to make matters worse for one another, because fighting and shit like that only do ourselves more harm than good. Both of us got hurt and sat in the hole. But hey, when your back was against the wall, and your only way out was to fight, what other choice do you have, and what are you going to do? Run to the deputy like a little bitch, or fight? I fought, but not yet. He was stalking me, waiting for me to slip, for more of his homeboys to get locked up. Now there were two of them. Still nothing till the shower; the water was ice cold, and I was shaking for fifteen minutes, with just the little towel around my waist, waiting for the inmate workers to throw out my jail clothing from the laundry. The place was sick. Butt naked, I got seated right behind the next man with someone else right behind me waiting to see the nurse before we were housed. It happened when we were done with the booking processing and were going up to the twin tower to our assigned housing but; before we got into the elevator, one of the homies swung—not the one that told me to watch my back, but the other one, the one that came later and didn't say shit. He swung, but I had been ready and waiting for the punch. So I ducked; using my right hand to block my face, I laid a smooth uppercut to his jaw, sending him trembling back, followed with a left hook. On seeing this, the loudmouth came charging. I swung my left leg back and took more of my body to one side to bring my elbow to shut the screaming little bitch up. Turning around, I brought the hard bone back to meet his homie-ass nose, and in that instant the guard was on my ass. It didn't last a minute. Both of 'em was on the ground before the guard came running.

And when they took me to the interview, I refused to talk when they questioned of who did what, so one of the deputy said, "Uh! You want to be a tough guy, ha? We'll see about that." So the skinny tweeker-look-alike motherfucker threw me into the lion's den. It was a house full of them. I'm not Daniel, so I got attacked by all twelve of the homies. I tried with all my might to fight 'em off, but there were too many of them, and they beat the daylight out of me; I went unconscious and woke up in a different cell with no other inmates besides myself. My head hurt, and my whole body ached. My ribs might have been broken. Both my eyes were swollen almost shut, I had one tooth missing and my lips busted in half, top and bottom. I went from good shape to bad, almost dead was more like it. I couldn't even eat. Every time I tried to swallow something, my throat hurt; even water was hard to go down, and water was my only diet. I lost weight quickly just within that week, all because I got put into the mix that I knew nothing about; by the time my transfer bus arrived, I lost twenty-five pounds, and I learned my lesson well about the LA Country Jail.

CHAPTER 90

Back on the bus, shaking from head to toe, my eyes were still swollen and glued shut. But I managed to see Melrose and a couple of other streets of LA, then I fell asleep from hunger and woke up at the Orange County Jail. The bus picked up a girl, then was back on the road to drop some prisoners off at Delano, and the girl that we picked up at Chowchilla on to 99, Merced, and it was night when we finally stopped in front of the Stanislaus County Jail; I was taken through the visiting and R and R door on the ground floor, instead of the regular underground entrance. From here it was "hurry up and wait." It was 4:00 AM before my name was called to be housed upstairs, and the second floor was where the general population was housed. The next day, as I was lying on my assigned bunk in east quarter 3, my name was called for a visit. And I knew it was only one person, and that was Sara, and my children. Cleaning myself up a little before going down, I was still unrecognizable; on entering the visiting room and upon setting her eyes on me, Sara thought I was someone else and almost walked out—I had to tap the window in time to get her attention and called her back with my hand. When she did, I showed her my wristband, and she asked me, "What happened?" I could barely talk, and all my children were worried about their father. For the first time in a long time, I cried and cried in front of my family, but all of them seemed to feel my pain, which in turn made me feel no shame and love them even more. Now I had something to live for. The visit was short, especially that I had a long story to tell, and a hard time telling it. It was so quick that I felt like they just walked in, and it was over. Sara reminded me to make sure I called her when I got back to my assigned housing, which I did, then hung up after remembering a reminder about waiting for late night to call, when everybody went to sleep and the phones were open. That was when I got on, and we talked until it was time for her to go to work. And after work, she came back to see me again. This time, everybody's face looked even sadder;

I tried to cheer them up, but to no avail. I really felt for my children. Sara was studying my wounds and told me to go see a doctor.

I told her, "Yeah! Yeah!" But I had to buy my own aspirin from the canteen. I lay in bed all day in pain, watched TV through the bar, and when I got bored, I picked up the Bible, which had become a part of my life after a couple of Psalms. I started writing a letter, which didn't reach Sara before I got released the following Monday, as when I went to court, the judge dismissed my case, because it was a mistake of a photo lineup.

CHAPTER 91

Before appearing in the courtroom to receive my charge from the judge, Delores pulled me out of the dungeon to have a talk with me. On setting her eyes on me, she, too, couldn't believe how I looked and asked, "What happen to you?" I told her of how I got beat up, but my desire to find out about my case was stronger, so I asked her about the case.

"So what's this all about?"

Delores went into the beige envelope with the copy of the warrants, studied it, and said, "Well! It looks to me, you have been picked out the photo lineup. I echo, an information has point you out. The report read, Asian male, aged 22-32 years old, 5'2"-5'10" in height, and weighed 120-175 lbs." After reading the report, she pondered, and while she did this, I glanced over to see the copy of the six photos in the lineup. One of them was me; another Asian was my homie from the Hit Squad gang and who was currently locked up at the time. And the other four photos were black and white; two of them, I grew up and went to school with, were black. Delores was thinking the same thing I was thinking. I asked her for the date that the offense was committed; once the date indicated of my innocence, I told her about my homie in prison. Delores found a way out for me. As soon as the court session began, Delores wasted no time. "Your Honor, I believe this case to be a discrimination against my client because I don't think that he has a fair lineup because if you look"—taking the copy of the photo lineup to the bailiff and continuing—"you see, Your Honor, the report and the lineup are off beat as the suspect was described as an Asian male, which couldn't be my client, and the other Asian, he's serving time right now, he happened to be sent to prison by the county long before the alleged case takes place, and if that's not bad enough, the detective put four other colored males to help narrow down who the informants gonna pick out, set my client up to be the perfect suspect.

"Your Honor"—she dragged her words a bit—"I would like this case to be dismissed." And the judge granted the dismissal. I wasn't released until 4:00 PM; from the county jail, I walked about five blocks to Sara Long's house on Sixth Street while she was still at work. And I didn't have no key to get inside the house with, so I snooped around to see if there was any window that might be left opened. Just my luck. Not even a full hour that I got out, the same detective I saw in court followed me home, and she arrested me for breaking and entering. I tried to explain that I lived there, but she didn't want to hear none of it and took me to the police station, having me sit in the little tank with my cuffs on till Sara got off work and went to the station; a business card was left for Sara. She was told that she can call the number on the card that the detective left behind on her door; she did so and bailed me out of trouble.

CHAPTER 92

Today, Sara felt kind of tired, too tired to go pick up the kids from the grandparents' house. She decided to leave them there and caught up on herself and her sleep. There was only the grandpa now, as the grandma already went first to wait for him in the abyss of hell, because she was an evil bitch when she was alive. Parking her car on Sixth St. at the usual spot, Sara got out dragging her legs. Coming to the door, the card caught her attention. She picked it up and read it, MPD Detective A. G. Willis. Her first thought was her children, so she quickly called. I didn't know what they talked about or what type of questions were asked. I was just glad that the little cell door opened, and I saw my Sara Long; she waited while the uniformed officer uncuffed my hands. It was as much of a surprise to her as to my self. And since it had been a while since we last made love, we both felt kind of shy about each other's body, but that was only in public; once inside the house, door closed behind us, things changed. We were touching, rubbing, and caressing each other's body all night long, exploring, mixing, and melting into each other, becoming one. The next day, Sara had to call in and use her sick day; when we finally got out of the house around noon, we went to pick up the children, and all of them were thrilled to see their father. And that was the happiest moment of my life; being united with my family was my greatest joy. A couple of days later, after going out together, I was home alone, lying around, watching the History Channel, when a knock at the door came. I pulled the curtains back to see who it was and saw Delores. I was like, "What the fuck she's doing here?" My case was already over.

"Tommy, how are you doing?" she greeted as I opened the door. When I didn't respond, she asked, "Uh! Can I come in?"

"Sure!" She bent at the knees a little to pick up the suitcase and let me see her cleavage. I showed her to a chair in the dining room, and I cleared the tabletop. Delores wasted no time and reached down to pull out a file. I took my seat and tried not to glance over to see what was inside the folder, but it was a certification paper of some type. I kind of remembered seeing it before. Oh yes! When Father Robert left me his will. Oh shit! Sammie had signed her will to me, Cryxtal, and Diamond. This girl, I really admire her; even when she was gone, she still took care of us.

"Okay! Tommy, you know what this is all about, right? It's a will that your wife has left for you, and your children, plus her insurance policy. Now tell me, who will this will go to just in case something happens to you?" she asked.

"My children," I told her, and she already knew Cryxtal and Diamond, but not the others. I was too stoned to speak, as memories of Sammie flooded my mind, and went with the motion of the paperwork. Once I was done with the paper signing, Delores asked me if she could do anything else for me before she left. I had forgotten about my FHRSS account for my children.

When she asked, "Is there anything else I can do for you?" I moved my head from side to side. "Please feel free to give me a ring. Besides, you owe me one, and when can we get together, and make up, ha?" my counselor wanted to know; usually I caught these hints in the lustful smile, but I was in too much delight of the financial security for my Cryxtal and Diamond that I was blind to see an opportunity to bust a nut. All smiling, she went out the door, and she kept looking back, all the way to her white BMW, maybe hoping that I would call her back so we could fuck or something.

CHAPTER 93

I told Sara Long about my will as I recalled telling her that I just wanted her to stay home and stay with the children without having to worry about our financial situation. I had 1.5 million dollars to my name at the time on paper, and if I just started with what I had, I would have been set for life just living off interest earnings and other stocks and bond options. But no, I had to have the big idea of being a big-shot Mr. Business Owner living in a brand-new home, driving a nice car, and that was what I did. I went out and bought us a one-million import/export oriental goods and food produce supermarket, which didn't take us long to go out of business due to no demand. So we were forced to accept our loss and move on. Sara had her AA in office administration and had talked me into burning all that I had.

As the gas price went up, so did our chance of losing everything; I decided to hold on to the little that I had left from the devastating loss. But Sara couldn't rest easy, knowing that I got money; because she had ambition, the hunger within her craved for the disastrous. We desired similar outcomes, so again we partnered up and got into the gas station business, which only got us broke. Your mother Sara Long's health was giving out, and she took her final breath to rest in peace. From what I got for the gas station of $333,000 when it was sold, it was not enough to cover her hospital bills even with her insurance. We were on the verge of losing everything, and we couldn't think fast enough to get us out of all that mess. I was already starting to feel that I was back to square one, feeling the need to do something fast, full of disappointment with myself for letting myself and my family down when I had my chance. I messed it all up at the moment; I didn't even have enough money to even publish my books, and in my children's FHRSS accounts, there was zero cent in all of them. "Fuck! Here I go again, me against the world." I had to come up with something, and without funds, there was nothing I could do about anything. I just wanted to surrender to my failure. I was tired of fighting, and I didn't want to battle no more. I was down, but I was not completely out though. There was still some dog left in me, and with what I had left, I was intent to fight or was trying. So I made plans for my comeback, only to have the world of another set of troubles come crushing on top of my already-heavy burden, which I couldn't lighten the load under to make it easy for myself. I was forced to fight my way out of the mess that I had created and put myself in, digging my way out of the ground only to come face-to-face with Sue Upchurch.

CHAPTER 94

Walking into the C's Candy Store on McHenry, Sue Upchurch was being greeted by the young clerk Claire. "Hi, I'm Claire, can I help you choose a gift?"

"Yeah, I like twelve red balloons and one white one. I'd also take the heart-shaped box of chocolate over the shelf there and two plastic red roses."

"These"—Claire points—"will be fine."

"Oh yeah! Let me see the card in the rack right there"—pointing to the glossy red lips that were displayed on the wall behind the cashier—"I'll take all these."

Claire rang it up and double-checked with, "Would that be all?" Sue paid for it with cash.

Inside the greeting card, Sue Upchurch wrote,

"My sweet Tommy, I want you to know that I been missing you, and from a distance, I come searching for you. The twelve balloons represent my love for you and the white one the purity of it. The roses are us, always red and forever together. Love always, Sue Upchurch. PS. Enjoy your surprise."

I was at home on the phone, trying to land me a "creating ads" job, when the front doorbell rang. For a second I thought it was my parole officer; I tried to think if I had done anything to violate—nothing. With the phone connected to my ear, I went to look out through the peephole. It was a relief when I saw only a delivery boy in a chocolate and white colored striped uniform with the C's Candy logo. On opening the door, the nice young man, who was probably still in school, said, "Hi, I, uh, have a delivery for Mr. Tommy Ok?" I pointed to myself while talking on the phone at the same time with my potential employer. He handed me the clipboard to sign. I scribbled my name and handed the clipboard back to the delivery boy. He tore off the receipt and handed it to me. I threw the delivery boy a thumbs-up as I was trying to conduct my phone conversation.

"Two o'clock, yes, 2:00 PM will be fine. I'll bring my portfolio. Okay! I'll see you then. Thank you." Then I hung up. Sitting at home alone, I felt sorry for my chickenshit-ass self. I couldn't believe that what I had tried to avoid all my life had finally come to haunt me. I had my chance and messed it all up. The ruts of nine to five were my deepest fears, but it caught up on me, and I had to face reality. I kept taking deep sighs, with my heart pounding outta line; heading myself onto the couch after hanging up the phone, I picked up the note that was attached to the floating air balloons. It read, "To Tommy Ok, from Sue Upchurch," and the first thing that came to my mind was, "Here comes trouble. Fuckin' bitch." With hostility, I ripped the envelope open to see a card with a woman's lips, and the words read, "This kiss is for you." Inside I read what she wrote, and I got even hotter; burning in rage, I let out "Fuck!" in between clenched teeth! Pulling the box of chocolates, I tore the wrapping open, and I started to pop the variety of sweets into my mouth, lying on the couch to go back to what I was doing, going over the portfolio that Sara had put together for me; she did a good job on it. Going through the yellow pages at the same time, I couldn't believe I was looking for a job. I knew I had to do something to get back on the ground I once stood on. But what was I about to do? It takes money to make money in America, and so far, I wasted all mine and made none in return.

CHAPTER 95

Waiting for Sara and the children seemed kind of longer than usual that day. And for some strange reason, with every piece of candy that went in my mouth, the more sick I felt to my stomach. I tried to blame it on the morning coffee that sometimes made me wanna shit. But it couldn't be, because coffee never made me blurry before. What was sweet was now bitter to my taste buds. I was like, "What the fuck?" so I set the box of chocolates aside, hoping that what was bothering my stomach would go away by the time my family returned from school. But my stomach only got worse by the second; now, I felt like I needed to go take a shit or puke. My system was rejecting everything, even water. I tried to think of what was it that I ate. I didn't recall drinking; maybe food poison, I told myself. The pain came again. I wanted to wait for Sara to get home before doing anything. But for some odd reason, she seemed to take her sweet candy-ass time. So for the first time in my life, I dialed 911, and it was for my self. I couldn't take this upside down and inside out, spinning and flipping. I felt hot and chill, felt like passing out, like my spirit was ready to go out of my body. My legs were already turning into water under me, sending me to the ground as I tried to reach the bathroom to use the toilet and throw up. I knew I had to go into the emergency room, as I had a feeling that I had been poisoned. I could feel it in my stomach. I kept on repeating, "Ambulance, Ambulance." I was suffocating; all air had escaped my lungs. I don't remember how long I stayed unconscious before the knock on the screen, followed by the doorbell ringing, and I knew who it was—my family! In desperation, I screamed at the top of my lungs to the point that it pained me, and I barely heard my own self as the sound that came out of my mouth was so low, cursing myself for being in that position. But then again this was America, and who would pay attention to such small things as candies? I felt like going out again, this time stronger. The light flooded the room as the door flew open, with shadows of two officers of some type. The room was spinning, hands sweaty, and perspiration started to form. From somewhere I heard the siren, and it was getting closer and went off altogether.

I heard my children calling me, "Daddy! Daddy!" Then came the EMT, rushing in with a stretcher—at least that's what I thought the uniformed officers were. I felt my body was being raised, and I was going up. I didn't want to fall. "No!" I yelled, and I tried to fight and tried hard. I tried to stop them, but I couldn't move as I kept going higher and higher till my body crushed against the moon. I prayed to God for him to help me get over this intoxication; bouncing off the stars and out deeper into space, I kept on floating. There were bright stars and lights flashing the colors of rainbow. I wanted to say it was beautiful, but at the same time it was like something I had seen before; why was it leading me into some kind of tunnel? And the earth moved and shook; I felt like I was on water, losing faith in the same way that Peter did, and starting to go down? I was scared out of my soul. I screamed for help, but no help came as I was going into the darkness. The world was devoid of everything. I didn't want to die, and I cried for Sara Long and all of my children. I wanted to see their faces one last time. And I was out. This was all that I can remember, before the world went blank on me.

CHAPTER 96

After my stomach was finished being pumped of the Castrol beans that Sue Upchurch tried to poison me with, coming back to myself and out of the ICU, I would say it was about noontime, and the day was beautiful with the shining sun bright, the rays bouncing off, the leaves glittering, sparkling, the green color of the tree making it come alive. I was looking through the parted curtain; I also saw and thanked God. The IV tube was cutting through my nose, mouth, and there was a needle in my arm, but slowly the room tucked. I was surrounded by Sara and my children; I called for all of them. "I want all of you to come closer," I ordered. They all obeyed and got closer. Once all of them did, I started, "Do you remember what your father tell you, what and how each and every one of you mean to me?"

Elisabeth, bravely blessing the day, spoke enough, and I got up. "I'm your first born, and first love."

"How about you, Alexandria? Where are you? Why are all of you don't want to come close? If that's the case, go away."

"Tommy! Hang in there, honey!" I did, with disappointment weighing on my heart, so I let what was inside of my chest off.

"Sara, there's something that I have to let you know. When I was in Lawton, Oklahoma, me and this nun/professor, Sue Upchurch—she was my tutor before we got involved after the death of my first love, future wife that are not meant to be, Kimberly." On hearing this, there was disappointment in Sara's eyes, also disbelief and distrust, but I didn't care because the truth stood, and sometimes the truth hurt. But hey! Better now or never, so you could deal with it before it was too late. "After my wife's death, Father Robert asked Sue Upchurch to tutor me with my speech and communication. Even though I was on the rebound. But I don't think it's me. A poor lonely terrestrial with a crashed plan, hope, and broken dreams, and got taken advantage of. She molested me. Yes, she took advantage of me and raped me. It happened again and again till we got caught doing it in the church bathroom." I probably offended Sara, and with tears, she said she forgave me.

"Anyway, when I ran out on her at first to get away and then, the second time and that's when I think she turned from beautiful to evil, and now she's coming after me, to kill me and anyone else that is connected to me because she promised me that that's what she'll do. This accident I believe was fixed and crafted by her." But Sara didn't seem surprised, and it showed; I did my best to describe Sue Upchurch and turned my attention back to my children to continue with what we were talking about—how much they meant to me, especially Cryxtal and Diamond, because if I left them, they would be alone and without help. I told my children to be on alarm about a white lady, stay alert, and watch out for a white female who might appear strange or being too nice out of the ordinary.

CHAPTER 97

Coming to see me was the law officer from the PD to investigate about what happened—two uniformed officers and one plainclothes detective. Their target suspect was Sara, and as soon as they saw her, the detective flashed his badge and introduced himself as Detective Whatever-the-fuck-his-name-was-B-some-shit. "Excuse me, miss, are you Sara Long?" he asked after the introduction of flashing his badge and of stating who they were and were working for; he tried to throw Sara off guard. For some strange reason, tears seemed to choke her up, making her unable to speak and only nodding her head back at the detective. "Miss Long, let me inform you that I am only doing my routine investigation, so if you can come to the Modesto Police Station with us, I would greatly appreciate your cooperation." Lying-ass punks. She was already the prime suspect, guilty before proving any guilt. "We only have some question to ask you." The detective tried to get Sara to relax and be comfortable by allowing her to take the front seat of his cruiser. Sara was still nervous because she had never been this close to any law enforcement officer before. She was hella uncomfortable, and the drive was so long; and her mind was full of me, trying to piece things together as to what had happened, occasionally distracted by the dispatch on the radio. Once the car was parked, the detective led her to the station. Going up the stairs, they made a right turn, and she was being ushered into one of the small rooms. With camera recorders sitting on top of the corners of the many empty rooms, the detective first went to speak with the captain. And once he got the okay, the detective started the investigation, and the interrogation began. After a few straight questions and answers, that was all it took for the detective to be convinced and to place Sara under arrest. "Mrs. Long, I'm afraid I have to place you under arrest for attempted murder, trying to poison your boyfriend. I want you to understand that you have the right to remain silent. You have a right to a lawyer present before speaking with us. Because anything you say can, and will be used against you in the court of law." On hearing her rights, Sara spoke up and cut the detective short.

"Look! I don't need a damn lawyer because I believe you are gravely mistaken. Only if you know how much I love my Tommy, please save yourself the embarrassment and the possibility of demoding?"

"Yeah! You love him enough to try and poison him for his money," the detective mocked her. "Besides, when the juries find you guilty, Tommy's going to love you even more." The detective was all smiling, not knowing that he made a bad decision.

CHAPTER 98

Elisabeth and the siblings were still at my bedside, but all of them were ready to go home; but they wanted to wait for Sara to return first as the B-some-shit-whatever-the-fuck-his-name was told 'em, but she never showed back up after she was taken to the police station, and I hoped she was okay. I told Elisabeth to call a cab and go home to wait for their mother. "Your brothers and sisters are tired," I told Elizabeth. So she called a cab, because it was late, something like past 2:00 AM. Residing at Oakdale, named Steve, the nice cabdriver came to the service of transportation, and when my children got inside the house, there was a surprise waiting as soon as the door clicked open and then closed. Sue Upchurch stepped out to block the door and in a soft tone said, "Hello! My children, come to Mommy."

On seeing the white female, Elisabeth remembered my warning and bravely asked, "What are you doing here, and what are you planning to do with us?" All five siblings were glued together like baby chicks without their mother hen. They were fearful and frightened out of their wits. But Elisabeth was standing up for what she felt was her responsibility and the right thing to do, and that was to fight for them, only to find all five of them tied up and thrown into the bathroom. There was the window, but also the bars. So hopeless, all five of them, sitting in-line along the tub, lucky the detective decided to come back and speak to me at the hospital, and that was when I told him everything about Sue and her motive. And at that instant, he knew that his actions were not out of his better judgment. So he called in and asked for some protection to be sent to aid my children. I heard him give the dispatcher my address and request for the release of Sara Long, which was done. And one of the uniformed sheriffs was giving her a lift in his patrol car to the house. With the call from the dispatch, he switched on his light, without using the siren. He was racing to the house.

Chapter 99

Just sitting there silently thinking, Elisabeth recalled helping her mother hide a little gun that looked almost like a toy, a .22 pearl handle, and it was behind the wall outlet. On realizing this, she quickly looked around for a screwdriver to take out the plastic cover. But she found nothing and had to make do with the little scissor that she found with both hands still tied in front of her. She worked the screw to the best that she knew how. Once it came off, she had another problem. She couldn't reach her hand in to retrieve the weapon, and by the time she thought about freeing her hands with the scissor, it was already too late. Sue Upchurch had come back and checked on them. And on seeing the scissor in Elisabeth's tied hand, she went in rage and slapped Elisabeth across her face, telling her, "You are a bad girl. Who taught you to be disobedient? Looks like I'm going to have to teach you some manners." Sue's hand was in midair about to strike, when a knock at the door got her attention, and she stopped with her disciplining.

Then the voice came, "This is the police, you can open up." And the two uniformed officers waited a little too long for someone to come to the door, before they decided to kick down the door. On the first thump, Sue jumped up to attention. Taking one last look at all five children, she started to make her way out, heading for the sliding door that led to the backyard from the main kitchen.

On seeing that Sue was running, Alexandria yelled out, "Help! Help! Help!" Soon all five of them joined in and yelled out for help. The door flew open on the third attempt, with their guns already drawn. They swept side to side toward where the screaming for help of the siblings were coming from. Signaling his partner with his hand signs, the two officers checked the whole house; the backup arrived.

The detective raced to the house, reached my children, and comforted them with, "It's okay! You do remember me from the hospital, right?" They did, and he managed to get the siblings to calm down and relax a bit from their terror. The detective showed his appreciation by thanking them, "Thank you, little ones, for saving my butt. Today, you are my hero, and to reward you, your mommy's outside." Sara Long was frightened and as terrified as the children, scared to death that something might have happened to her babies. Upon seeing all of them, she cried with joy as all her babies were brought out to her by the Detective B-some-shit-whatever-the-fuck-his-name-was. Running to them, she took all of them into her arms. To make amends, the detective offered them a ride to the hospital to see me.

CHAPTER 100

When the detective got to my bedside, I had just currently been informed that I could go home by my nurse, and hating doctors as is, I got out of the hospital as quickly as I was allowed to be out. It had been busy for the family, making time impossible for each other, and we actually spent quality time together, with Sara Long regretting the fact about you. God wanted me to go to our unborn child first, but the truth of the matter was, Sara Long needed me here with her more than our dead baby in the abyss. But like they said, "God don't like ugly people." The baby was three months old when Sara took the baby out of her body; and from that date, exactly thirty years later, your mother had a tumor in her stomach and died. I was at the funeral, but I left early as I couldn't bring myself to face all of you.

CHAPTER 101

The reason why I keep coming in and out of all your lives, it's not that I don't love you. It's because of the fact that I love all of you; that's why I keep on coming and going to check up and make sure you're okay. Because I care; besides, from what my eyes can see from my own fruits and tribulations, if I didn't have no parent or parents and managed to make it far, I know that all of you will be all right with your mother's help, while I go on my own separate way so I can take care of business without any distraction. I have to admit that there's no place on earth worse than around where I once was standing on. From when I left you, I was down to only my bus ticket, one way at that, armed with a backpack full of unpublished books. I knew not a damn thing to do, but I understood what I needed to do, and that was to self-publish my book. Which I did, and my first book printed was and is a success, *Diamond Boy*, selling faster than the press can spit it out; and just like you, I gained my ground back, but your outcome is better than your old man's, which makes me proud of all of you, especially my Diamond Boy. And it was after my success that I came to see that America is what you want to make it, because this is the land of the free, with plenty of opportunities, for anything that anyone wants to do can be accomplished. All it takes is a good plan, and work the plan good. Plus a little willpower and determination, your dreams in America will turn into reality, because the sky is the limit. I came out of the mist of the killing field, so I know you are in paradise on earth's greater society. Life in America shouldn't have any problem or any reason not to be successful. It's all up to you to make embellishments and create and mold your destiny.

CHAPTER 102

"Now, my children, my time has come, now please let me be on my way, because I need going back to where I come from, so I can start the good deed that I have in my heart to do long ago, that America had made possible now for me to learn and to do and receive my doctor's degree, and the Bible is my medicine kit. I'm not out to save lives, but save souls; not to care after flesh wounds, but the wounded spirit, and heal the broken hearts. Sharing the good news where it hasn't been told is my goal. I understand why Father Robert wanted me to read the Bible over and over again because he knows that no one man can completely know the Bible. There's always something new, and exciting, and at times lifts you up to the sky and that's the high I want, the holy taken back to my people. Is there something else that I haven't said and that you want to know about?"

"How about that Sue Chrunch girl?" Johnathan asked.

"You mean Sue Upchurch?" I corrected him.

"Yeah! That girl. The one that tied us up. You never said anything about her besides she's coming to try."

"Johnathan, stop. That girl is a long story by herself," I conceded, "but for you, my children, anything at all I'll do, and in return, I want you to let me be on my way once I'm done. Is anyone else besides Johnathan interested in hearing about Sue?" Nobody moved, a sign that they gave me their full attention, for me to continue with them now. "Was a good nun who turned bad, doing the unthinkable, ugly things, and changing good deeds."

CHAPTER 103

My Cryxtal spoke up for the first time. "And where were you going all this time when you were away?" she wanted to know, and stupid me forgot to let my children know that I went back to school to continue my Bible theology education with Crossroads Institute; and now that I had the qualification, I was ready to do the great thing that I was destined to do, which I didn't think I could get anywhere else but here in America. And if you want to compare my gain between the money I made from writing and the knowledge of the Bible, I dare to say there are no riches accumulating that are better than the treasures found inside the Holy Bible. There is no comparison to the riches I gained from the treasure that's inside the Bible. So I'm going back to Cambodia with my wealth, to enlighten those spirits that are once like mine—poor, starving, and longing to be set free. I paused. "You mean you got your doctor degree in Bible teaching?" my Cryxtal wanted to be clear.

"Yes, my daughter, and I don't think there is no other profession like it because the Bible is the combination of everything the Master created to unlock everything. Once I understood Father Robert's purpose, I decided I want to be like my father who is watching over me right now."

Chapter 104

Map, Sammie's brother in Lowell, went into his used-car lot business, only to lose everything he got as the location was too close to the highway; and the saltwater flying from the freeway got the cars rusted faster than he can find buyers to purchase them, along with not enough consumers shopping, and a clientele not ready to buy. Map's business came and went down the drain, forcing him to file bankruptcy, sending him back to his place of slaving from nine to five to support his family of five, the result from his loss. I learned that experience goes a long way, making you know what you're doing. Mr. Cooper's experience had predicted a truth that in life you have to be in the know of things and what you are doing. We stayed in touch even though we were not the best of in-laws; at least I have a brother-in-law. I owe him that much, to never lose contact, because who knows, this is America; one day he might help bury me, or I help bury him, and that's just the way it is. Life is very unpredictable living in America.